Reading in Early Childhood

READING IN
EARLY CHILDHOOD
A Linguistic Study of a Preschool Child's
Gradual Acquisition of Reading Ability

Ragnhild Söderbergh

FOREWORD BY THEODORE ANDERSSON
INTRODUCTION BY ROBERT LADO

GEORGETOWN UNIVERSITY PRESS
WASHINGTON, D.C.

Library of Congress Cataloging in Publication Data

Söderbergh, Ragnhild.
    Reading in early childhood.

    Bibliography: p.
    1. Reading (Preschool) 2. Reading readiness.
3. Education, Preschool—Sweden—1965——   I. Title.
LB1140.5.R4S6 1976   372.4'09485   76-43032
ISBN 0–87840–165–2

International Standard Book Number: 0-87840-165-2

to

Elias Wessén

CONTENTS

FOREWORD

One day in 1970, as I was leafing through a catalog of Aguilar, the well-known Madrid publisher, my eye alighted on a fetching picture of a baby, and I read 'Los bebés pueden leer' (Babies can read). These intriguing words led me into the description of a book titled *Cómo enseñar a leer a su bebé*, by one Glenn Doman. Assuming this to be a translation, I had no difficulty in finding the original in the university library under the title *How to Teach Your Baby to Read: The Gentle Revolution* (Random House, 1964). I devoured the book with complete suspension of disbelief owing, I suppose, to the fact that it seemed to confirm my still embryonic hunches.

This was the beginning of my interest in early reading (ER); but when I sought to share my enthusiasm with my colleagues specializing in reading, I met with politeness (for we were in Texas), but also with glassy eyes. When later I asked Glenn Doman why he was not better known among academics, he replied that he was addressing his message not to academics, who are more given to talk than to action, but rather to mothers, who are highly motivated to raise their children in the best way they can. And so I discovered the distance separating the two worlds, that of academics and that of mothers, both concerned with children's education but rarely communicating. One exception, however, is worth noting: the St. Lambert experiment outside Montreal, where mothers of English-speaking children persuaded Wallace Lambert, Professor of Psychology at McGill University, to undertake an immersion program in French from kindergarten through the elementary grades, a program which has proved to be outstandingly successful. (See Wallace E. Lambert and G. Richard Tucker, *Bilingual Education of Children*, Rowley, Massachusetts: Newberry House Publishers, 1972.)

Only a few weeks after my discovery of Doman I got a letter from

Ragnhild Söderbergh, then Docent (Associate Professor) of Linguistics and now Professor of Child Language at the University of Stockholm. She informed me that she had taught her daughter to read (Swedish) between the ages of 2.4 and 3.6, using the Doman method. In due course she sent me a copy of her book, written in English, in which she relates in detail and from the point of view of a linguist her daughter's 'gradual acquisition of reading ability.' The experiment was successfully replicated with five other Swedish children between the ages of one and a half and three years (see her *Project Early Reading: A Theoretical Investigation and the Practical Application*, Stockholm: University of Stockholm, Institute of Scandinavian Languages, 1973). She also sent me two papers for a Conference on Child Language which I was organizing and which took place in Chicago in November, 1971: 'A Linguistic Study of a Swedish Preschool Child's Gradual Acquisition of Reading Ability' and 'Swedish Children's Acquisition of Syntax: A Preliminary Report.' (See Theodore Andersson and William F. Mackey, eds., *Bilingualism in Early Childhood: Proceedings of a Conference on Child Language, Chicago; November 22–24, 1971,* Québec: Presses de l'Université de Laval, forthcoming.)

Ragnhild Söderbergh's book, originally published in 1971 but quickly sold out, fills a very special need. Its scientific precision is likely to reassure the academics who find Doman's tone too popular. At the same time it should appeal to thoughtful parents, for the author writes both as a scientist and as a mother. Her writing is at once theoretically sound and satisfying concrete and practical.

It is also timely. No fewer than four books have appeared in 1975 which directly or indirectly relate to early reading.

Donald G. Emery, a former superintendent of schools in Scarsdale, New York, and Shaker Heights, Ohio; a former director of the National Reading Center in Washington, D.C.; and at present Assistant Superintendent for Instructional Services for the Board of Cooperative Educational Services in Westchester County, New York, contends, cautiously, that 'most children are ready to learn to read at four' and that parents can teach their preschool children to read successfully— and enjoy it. (See *Teach your Preschooler to Read,* New York: Simon and Schuster, 1975.)

Sidney Ledson, a Canadian free-lance educator, writer, and artist, recounts in his book *Teach Your Child to Read in 60 Days* (New York: W.W. Norton, 1975) how 'he taught his two daughters, aged two and a half and four, to read, improvising the system as they went along.' Ledson's title does not inspire confidence; and in fact, despite the great amount of time and ingenuity devoted to the task, the author did not really teach his daughters to read in sixty days. They did have a reading vocabulary of 186 words; and in the next sixty days, partly with the assistance of a young girl who monitored their reading, they increased their reading vocabulary rapidly and began reading books, first with help and then on their own.

Wood Smethurst, an Ed.D. from Harvard University, now teaching at Emory University, who has had experience teaching reading to two- to five-year-old children, offers engagingly to help parents 'who want to help their preschoolers learn about reading.' He contends that 'a first-grade classroom is by no means the only place for a child to begin reading—and maybe it is not even the best place.' He makes it clear that he will not *'persuade any parent to teach any child.'* Addressing parents, he says, 'The choice is entirely yours: if you want to, if your child wants to, I can suggest several ways to go about it.'

Burton L. White, Project Director and Principal Investigator for the Preschool Project of Harvard University's Graduate School of Education, has summarized some seventeen years of research with young children in his important book *The First Three Years of Life* (Englewood Cliffs, N.J.: Prentice-Hall, 1975). He believes that 'the educational developments that take place in the year or so that begins when a child is about eight months old are *the most important and most in need of attention of any that occur in human life*' (pp. 129–130). Despite this conclusion, Burton White takes a firm position with the academic establishment: 'I do not think the reading kits that are commercially available and claim to get children on the road to reading at eight and nine months of age should be used. I believe strong statements to the effect that you *must* read stories to your child, and that you *must* buy as many "educational" toys as you can are examples of exploitation of the insecurities of American families. . . .' (pp. 145–146).

Among these somewhat conflicting views, Ragnhild Söderbergh adopts a scholarly position. Like Smethurst, she refrains from persuading her readers, and yet by describing minutely how one child did in fact learn to read, she allows her example to encourage other parents to undertake a similar venture if they feel so inclined. Unlike White, she is not afraid to encourage early reading, but like White she understands that it must be done without pressure, for the fun of it. She is the one who observes the process of early reading most closely and who analyzes it most scientifically. It is her book, therefore, that has the best chance of bringing together the world of educators and the world of mothers in this still controversial field of early reading.

THEODORE ANDERSSON
Professor of Spanish and Education

The University of Texas
at Austin

INTRODUCTION
The Significance of Söderbergh's
Reading in Early Childhood

My encounter with early reading was first theoretical as a linguist (personal notes 1967) and later agonizingly practical as parent of a deaf child (1972). As a linguist I wrote in my notes that if a child has the mental maturity to learn to speak and understand, he also has the mental maturity to learn to read; and he can learn, provided his visual development is on a par with his auditory one.

As a parent, when delay in the onset of language development in our youngest child raised the question of deafness and when subsequent auditory tests confirmed a severe to profound hearing loss, I felt compelled to try early reading as a way to bring the child into contact with language. With auditory training in preschool, plus the early reading experience at home, the child succeeded in learning to speak and to read, and she is at present attending third grade in a public school for normal hearing children, with support from a specialist during one period a day. Furthermore, this child is the best reader among her brothers and sisters at the same age.

As a parent I also used early reading techniques developed for the deaf child with a normal hearing child who had to repeat first grade largely because of problems in learning to read. Later, I found Doman's *Teach Your Baby to Read* (1964) and still later Söderbergh's *Reading in Early Childhood* (1971). Doman had already presented the idea that very small children can learn to read, and he described a method by which even brain-injured children were learning to read.

Söderbergh's study, an ordered and detailed linguistic experiment in which she taught her daughter Astrid to read between the ages of 2 years, 4 months and 3 years, 5 months, is significant to linguists and psycholinguists for four reasons. (1) It is the first full linguistic study of a case of reading acquisition. As such it seeks out and presents specific data systematically and interprets the data as part of acquiring a linguistic code. The interpretations are commensurate with the data observed, neither going beyond nor ignoring any of it.

(2) Her study is significant because Söderbergh succeeds as a trained linguist in implementing an experimental linguistic method adapted to the study of early reading. This method includes the control of input under experimental conditions to test whether or not the child will acquire the code through experience in reading without specific formal teaching of the code itself, parallel to the way the child acquires and develops language. Because exposure to reading is less pervasive than exposure to spoken language, the method permits much greater control of reading input; and Söderbergh's interpretations are more likely to explain adequately the effect of the experimental reading sessions.

She observes the child's strategies in attacking new words and classifies them into misidentifications, analytical reading, and non-readings; and she further analyses the analytical readings convincingly into the linguistic processes of adjunction, deletion, and substitution. The analysis proceeds from words to morphemes, and, as the strategies of the child evolve, progresses to graphematic readings, which after fourteen months result in the child's tacit knowledge of the graphophonematic correspondences of Swedish. This tacit knowledge permits her to read any new word and to decode the written message contained in sentences.

(3) Söderbergh is able to relate her experiment to linguistic views and research on beginning reading, and to psycholinguistic findings on language acquisition. She is also able to refer to the current views and debates among reading specialists.

(4) If we view early reading as language acquisition in the receptive mode of language processing through its written form, the experiment has great methodological interest for the study of language development since it permits a more complete record of input than do studies of spoken language acquisition, as well as a more complete record of output. The researcher in early reading can log every new word or sentence presented to the child and can record almost all the readings

performed by the child. In oral language acquisition the researcher usually observes the child for limited periods of time, and even when techniques of elicitation are used to obtain an adequate sample of the child's performance, the observations may still be incomplete.

Reading in Early Childhood is therefore a landmark for those who are doing research on early reading and language acquisition and as such it is of interest to linguists and psycholinguists in general.

For parents and teachers it also does significant things. (1) It shows that one can teach a child to read at home before he enters school and it shows one successful way of doing it. Since Swedish spelling complexities are comparable to those of English in difficulty, Söderbergh's success should be a source of encouragement for those who wish to work with English.

(2) The study opens up a potentially beneficial side effect of early reading on the vexing problem of spelling ability. Söderbergh reports that Astrid's spelling had become 'remarkably good' by age four and a half. And, 'Now, at the age of seven and a half she simply knows how to spell and needs not devote any time to learning how. This skill, which is normally attained only after many years of hard school work, had come to her quite unconsciously as a by-product of her early reading.' (pp. 118–119)

Writing and spelling are usually nonmotivational subjects in school and tedious home assignments in most cases. And little wonder. Let us imagine what it would be like for school children to struggle with speaking as they struggle with spelling and writing. It would be sheer torture if, every time the child tried to say something, he had to ponder how to pronounce each word (with *b* or *v*, with *w* or *h*) and if he had to go to the dictionary to find out how to pronounce the words he used, scores of them. Yet that is what takes place when children do their writing assignments at present, and when they have their spelling lessons and do their spelling homework.

'Would it not be a good thing,' asks Söderbergh, 'if all children had this experience: of learning to read as easily as they learn to talk and of learning to spell without knowing that they are learning how: of having attained full literacy at an age when children normally begin to learn the ABC? During the first school years a lot of time and hard work is now being devoted to acquiring the elementary skills of

reading and spelling. With these skills already at the pupil's command there could be time for more meaningful and stimulating work
and activities at school.' (p. 119)

Could it be that the answer to Rudolf Flesch's challenge in his
book, *Why Johnny Can't Read* (1955), and the parallel problem of
why Johnny can't spell, is not a matter of phonics but of age? Some of
us think that it might well be. All of us, teachers, parents, reading
specialists, linguists, and psycholinguists owe it to the children to
find out. Söderbergh, in *Reading in Early Childhood,* has broken the
ground in a scholarly as well as a practical way.

ROBERT LADO
Professor of Linguistics

Georgetown University
School of Languages and Linguistics

PREFACE

This book is a *linguistic* study of a child's gradual acquisition of reading ability. I have closely studied a child learning to read from the age of two years and four months by the so-called Doman method—by learning whole words as entities. I have shown how the child, as it learns more and more words, gradually breaks down these words into smaller units: first morphemes, then graphemes. At last the child arrives at an understanding of the correspondences between sound (phoneme) and letter (grapheme) and is able to read any new word through analysis and synthesis.

The findings of this study have been viewed in the light of recent linguistic theories as presented by research workers in child language inspired by Chomsky—such as Brown, Bellugi, Lenneberg.

Research in reading has so far been carried out mainly by psychologists and pedagogues; many of them have devoted a life-time to investigations in this field. It is not due to neglect of this research work that I have only casually referred to it in my book (this casualness will be evident to the expert consulting my bibliography, where many great names within psychology are lacking). Being a linguist I have deliberately refrained from intruding upon the ground of pedagogy and psychology. I hoped that by keeping as much as possible within my own field I might make a better contribution to the common fund of knowledge. My opinion is that research does not profit from linguists trying to become psychologists or vice versa, but from *co-operation of research workers from both sides*. In this preliminary study such cooperation has not been possible, but I here strongly stress what I say in Chapter Eleven: the broader study that ought to follow must be *a team work carried out by psychologists and linguists*.

The child studied in this book was an early speaker. She talked in two-word sentences from one year and four months and she actively mastered all the phonemes of Swedish except for /ɧ/ and /ç/ about the age of two years and six months. The phonemes /ɧ/ and /ç/ were mastered in November 1966, the month after the code had been broken. The girl was then three years and six months old.

For the benefit of those readers who do not know Swedish, this book has been provided with a glossary, where all Swedish words used in the book have been rendered in English. (Names have not been listed, however.) The alphabetical order follows Swedish conventions.

It is a great pleasure for me to have the opportunity of thanking everybody who has been directly or indirectly involved in making this book possible. Professor Karl-Hampus Dahlstedt and Professor Bengt Sigurd have helped me to get this study published. Professor Dahlstedt has also read the manuscript and contributed much valuable criticism. Docent Sture Allén has kindly allowed me to publish a graph of his on the distinctive features of Swedish syngraphemes.

George Simpson, M.A., has scrutinized my English, Fil. Mag. Theodor Katz, Fil. Mag. Sven Lange and Fil. Mag. Åke Livstedt have helped with proof-reading. Last not least I thank my little daughter for her joyful collaboration.

This book has been dedicated to my dear teacher in the Scandinavian Languages, Professor Elias Wessén. Although this research work does not belong to his field, he encouraged me to work along these lines at a time when the study of child language was not yet in vogue in Sweden.

RAGNHILD SÖDERBERGH

Sollentuna

Reading in Early Childhood

Chapter One
Learning to read. Theories and methods confronted with different linguistic theories

The basic concern in the education of man is to teach the art of reading. Quite naturally there are many ideas about how this skill should be acquired. In Charles C. Fries's book *Linguistics and Reading* (1963) we get a survey of the discussion on the teaching of reading from 1551 to 1900. There we are confronted with all the methods still under debate: phonic methods, word methods, sentence methods etc.

Since the middle of our century the bulk of literature on the subject had acquired such proportions and the debate had become so ferocious in the English-speaking countries that a committee on research of reading was called together at Syracuse University (1959). One of the outcomes of that conference was a decision to sum up and evaluate the major research on beginning to read. Professor Jeanne Chall was commissioned with this task, and the result appeared (1967) in "Learning to Read. The Great Debate" with the subtitle "An inquiry into the science, art and ideology of old and new methods of teaching children to read 1910—1965".

From Chall's book we learn that the methods for teaching reading are legion. The two extreme contrasts, however, are represented by what might be called "the pure phonics method" and "the reading for meaning method". Most other reading methods lie somewhere in between those two, stressing both phonics and meaning but in varying proportions.

The pure phonics method implies that the pupil is taught the letters of the alphabet and the corresponding sounds. Then he is taught to read by "sounding and blending", i.e. he sounds out the new words and then synthesizes the sounds so that the right word is produced. In that way the reader does not get the meaning of the word until the process of synthesizing is completed. By this method stress is put on word analysis.

The sponsors of the reading-for-meaning method oppose this—as they think—unnatural and boring way of reading and instead teach whole words and sentences from the very beginning, thus giving their pupils at once the experience of what are the ultimate goals of reading: comprehension, appreciation and—finally—application.

In the pure phonics method the child is presented with the code and taught how to use it. In the extreme reading-for-meaning method the child is not taught the code. True reading ability, however, means that a person is able to read any word, i.e. also one that he has never seen written or printed before. In order to do this he must know the code. If he is not taught the code he must somehow find it out by himself. All persons having been taught to read by a pure reading-for-meaning method must thus have found out the code all by themselves—or still be analphabetic!

Up to 1920 the prevailing method of teaching reading in English-speaking countries was one of phonics. A reaction came in the 1920s, when "reading for meaning" gained ground. From the 1930s and on the prevailing method had the following characteristics (see Chall, p. 13—15). The vocabulary presented was based on a frequency principle. The pupils were not taught letters and their sound values until they could read whole words. The children were taught "structural analysis", i.e. to recognize small meaningful parts of words, such as prefixes, suffixes and roots, and the components of compound words.[1] Silent reading was stressed from the beginning, and isolated practice of phonics was avoided. In fact, phonics was supposed to be integrated with meaningful connected reading and was often used only as a last resort. The child should then not "sound and blend" but was supposed to identify new words by visual analysis and substitution. Very often, however, the method of attacking new words was one of intelligent guessing by combining the knowledge of letters with picture and meaning clues from the context. When a child could not read a word, he was often told to identify the first letter and get the meaning from the rest of the sentence.

Rather soon there came a reaction towards this neglect of the code and the letter-sound correspondences. The popular debate culminated after the appearance of Rudolf Flesch's *Why Johnny Can't Read* (1955) where all the blame for children's reading failure was put on the prevailing reading-for-meaning method, and a return to pure phonics was suggested.

The heat and fervour of the popular debate led to the above-mentioned conference at Syracuse University and to Chall's book. In this, summing up the bulk of investigations about beginning to read, Chall finds that there are strong reasons to support the demand for a heavier emphasis on code learning. Her conclusions from the existing

[1] Using modern linguistic terminology we should call that morphemic analysis.

research are: "Early stress on code learning . . . not only produces better word recognition and spelling, but also makes it easier for the child eventually to read with understanding "(p. 83).

Chall gained support for the view that an early acquisition of the code is necessary from the theoretical considerations of linguists, particularly *Leonard Bloomfield* and *Charles C. Fries*.

In two articles published in *Elementary English* (1942) Bloomfield argued that the chief task when teaching a child to read is to teach him the code. As the child already has a good command of the spoken language the stress need not be put on meaning: the reader inevitably will grasp the meaning when the code is broken. To teach the code one should begin with regularly spelled words, i.e. where a certain letter always stands for a certain sound. By presenting sentences like "A fat cat ran at a bad rat" we make it possible for the child to discover the relationships between sounds and letters all by himself. Bloomfield was opposed to "sounding and blending"; he wanted words to be read as wholes. When a child did not recognize a word he should spell it, not sound it.

A view that is very similar to Bloomfield's is held by *Charles C. Fries*. In 1963 Fries published *Linguistics and Reading*. This is a unique book, as it is the first serious attempt to bring the sum of linguistic knowledge to bear upon the problem of how to teach reading.

After a most useful Introduction which contains a summary of contents (p. XII), C. C. Fries in Chapter One gives a survey of past practice and theory in the teaching of reading from 1551 onwards. Chapter Two contains a descriptive survey of linguistic science from 1820 to 1960, Chapter Three deals with language as a code. In Chapter Four C. C. Fries makes an analysis of the nature of the reading process in the light of modern linguistic knowledge. Chapters Five and Six are devoted to phonemics and graphemics; Chapter Six is devoted specially to English spelling. In Chapter Seven Fries draws practical conclusions from the earlier chapters. He presents the kinds of materials and methods which should be used in the teaching of reading if we are to make a "linguistically sound approach" to the problem.

As to the reading process C. C. Fries says: "The process of receiving a message through 'talk' is a responding to the language signals of his (the listener's) native language code—language signals that make their contact with his nervous system by *sound vibrations through the ear*. The process of getting the same message (the same meanings) by 'reading' is a responding to *the same set of language signals* of the same language code, but language signals that make their contact with his nervous system by *light vibrations through the eye*. The message is the same; the language code is the same; *the language signals are the same* for both 'talking' and 'reading'. The only essential difference here is the fact that in 'talk' the means of connection to the human nervous system consists of patterns of graphic shapes stimulating nerves in the eye. All 'writing' is the substituting of patterns of graphic shapes to represent the language signals of a code for the patterns of sound waves that have been learned as representing the same language signals" (p. 119). "The process of learning to read in one's native language is *the process of transfer* from the auditory signs for language signals, which the child has already learned, to the new visual signs for the same signals. This process of transfer is not the learning of the language code or of a new language code; it is not the learning of a new or different set of language signals. It is not the learning of new 'words', or of new grammatical structures, or of new meanings. These are all matters of the language signals which he has on the whole already learned so well that he is not conscious of their use" (p. 120).

Fries's view here seems to be that there is absolute identity between the code of written language and the code of spoken language: "the language code is the same".

As to phonemics—graphemics Fries says: "An *alphabet* is a set of graphic shapes that can represent the separate vowel and consonant phonemes of the language. All *alphabets* are phonemically based, and the procedures of teaching the process of reading alphabetic writing must take into account this essential fact of the structural base of alphabetic writing" (p. 156).

Fries here is heavily stressing *the dependence of written language upon spoken*.

The identity of the codes of written and spoken language and the dependence of written language upon spoken form the foundation of Fries's practical recommendations in Chapter Seven. Teaching to read, according to C. C. Fries, must imply teaching the process of transfer from spoken to written language. This teaching should be done in two steps.

First a child must learn to *identify the letters*. These are learned in groups according to their distinctive features.

In spite of Fries's heavy stressing of the fact that "all alphabets are phonemically based" he must admit that the second step in teaching English children to read cannot be to teach the sound values of the letters.

"The English alphabet is phonemically based but it is not, as used for English, a 'phonemic alphabet' in the sense that there is only one letter symbol for each phoneme and only one phoneme for each letter symbol. *We cannot expect, therefore, to be able to match each letter of the English alphabet, as it occurs in the graphic representation of English word-patterns,* with an English phoneme" (p. 160). Instead the author recommends that next the child should learn to *recognize the spelling patterns* of English represented by carefully selected corresponding groups of words such as *man—mane— mean, dan — dane — dean, ban — bane — bean* etc.

These first two steps in learning to read are called "the transfer stage". The author also has two further stages: "the stage of productive reading" when "the significant identifying features of the graphic shapes themselves sink below the threshold of conscious attention" (p. 205) and "the stage of 'vivid imaginative realization' " which "begins when the reading process has become so automatic for the reader that he uses reading equally with or even more fully than the live language of speech in acquiring and assimilating new experience" (p. 208).

Fries takes for granted that the codes of the written and the spoken language are the same. He also stresses the dependence of written language upon spoken. Here he is in line with Bloomfield, who does not only consider written language as secondary to and dependent on spoken language, but who is apt to disregard written language altogether, from a scientific linguistic point of view. "Writing is not language but merely a way of recording language by means of visible marks" (*Language*, p. 21).

Bloomfield was the linguistic pioneer of his time, and his views dominated the opinions of many linguists during the 1940s and 1950s. Recently, however, the written language has been considered an object worthy of investigation independently of the corresponding spoken language. There has been a strong tendency among linguists towards stressing the differences between the two codes, differences not only on the phonemic—graphemic level but also as regards morphemics and syntax. Linguists have even claimed that written language should be considered *as a more or less independent system.*

The views on this matter are compared and discussed by *Sture Allén* in the second chapter of his treatise *Grafematisk analys som grundval för textedering.*[2] Allén (p. 17) cites *H. J. Uldall*[3] who states that speech and writing are used parallel to express the same language. Neither, however, might be considered as primary: "There is no indication, either systematically or historically, of any such relation between them, for although it is true that in the history of mankind generally, as far as we know it, speech preceded writing, it is not true that the present sound pattern preceded the present orthography". Further, Allén (p. 15—16) quotes *W. Nelson Francis,* who in *Graphemic Analysis of Late Middle English Manuscripts* (1962)[4] considers "that a written text may be something other than an inaccurate secondary visual representation of an actually or potentially spoken primary; in fact that it may be a sort of primary itself, with its own structure deriving from a separate system having a history of its own, closely related to but not directly dependent upon the spoken language".

Allén's own view is summed up in the following words: "The connection existing between a spoken language and its written counterpart is not direct and simple but so complicated that the two media should be looked upon as different entities" (p. 155).

In *Linguistics and English Grammar* (1965) *H. A. Gleason Jr* on p. 108 gives his opinions on speech and writing: "Consider the position of a scholar somewhere outside the English-speaking world. He has learned to read English easily and perhaps does so regularly. He corresponds with colleagues abroad using written English, and occasionally he writes a paper for one of the international scholarly periodicals. His own language is not widely known, so he writes in English. But he never learned to speak English, and is very ill at ease when anyone tries to speak it to him. For him, English, in effect, has no phonology. And yet it functions effectively; he is able to keep up with the literature of his discipline and to contribute to it, all by use of English. The English he uses has three systems: a writing system, a grammar and a semology. Without some such structure it would fail him. Written English functioning in isolation from spoken English is an aberrant phenomenon" but "its occurrence demonstrates that written English has three systems, much as does spoken English". As to these three systems Gleason states that "we must have a description of the writing system of English in its own terms, that is, of the basic units of the writing system, not of the phonemes" (p. 109). Moreover "Written English has its own grammar. It

---

[2] See Sture Allén, *Grafematisk analys som grundval för textedering* (Graphemic Analysis as a Basis for Text Editing), Gothenburg 1965, p. 22 ff.—Differences between spoken and written language are also noted by Fries, but he seems to neglect these facts when he makes the theoretical statements which are the basis for his practical redommendations.—For a full account of this matter see Allén's treatise and the literature there cited.

[3] *Speech and Writing,* Acta Linguistica IV, 1944, p. 11 ff.

[4] *Speculum* XXXVII (1962), p. 32 f.

is not exactly like that of spoken English, though in broad outlines and many details the resemblance is very close". When it comes to semology Gleason says that we know too little about the semology of both written English and spoken English to be able to say how similar they may be.

Thus Gleason, like Allén, Francis and others, looks upon a spoken language and its written counterpart as different entities, each with its own structure. *Fries doesn't, however.*

Now if we accept the views of Allén, Gleason and others, and consider the written language as a more or less independent system, we might also say that learning to read is in fact like learning a new language.

The current trend in linguistics represented by Chomsky and his school has more or less revolutionized the ideas about language learning and language acquisition. According to Chomsky we have a biologically founded innate capacity for language. This means that when a child is exposed to language it does not just imitate but attacks the language he is being exposed to, observing it and constructing hypotheses about it. He builds his own model of the language, working out his own linguistic system consisting of sets of rules which are gross approximations of the correct system. As he is exposed to more and more linguistic material and as he is able to test his model by actual use of the rules when speaking, these rules are continually reconstructed and modified until, finally, the model becomes identical with the normal adult model. Chomsky's theories have been partly verified by many studies on child language presented during the 1960s, by Robert Brown, Ursula Bellugi, Colin Fraser, Paula Menyuk and others.[5] Belief in the biological foundations of language has been convincingly advocated also by Lenneberg in a book so titled which appeared in 1967.[5a] According to Lenneberg it is undisputable that the onset of speech and of certain linguistic abilities such as babbling, speaking isolated words, producing two word sentences etc. are determined by maturational processes (p. 127 f.).

The maturational processes and the innate capacity that cause children to start learning to speak at a certain age (18—28 months) without any form of instruction—the only requirement being that they are exposed to language—should also explain why this highly complicated learning process is being completed so quickly: within a period of two years all basic syntactic constructions of the language are mastered by the child.

Now, if a child learns to talk at a certain age without formal instruc-

[5] See Bibliography.
[5a] Eric H. Lenneberg *Biological Foundations of Language.*

tion, solely by being exposed to language, and if written language is to be considered as an independent system, why cannot a child learn to read *at the same age and in the same way* as he is learning to talk, solely by being exposed to written language? He would then be supposed to attack the written material, forming hypotheses, building models, all by himself discovering the code of the written language,[6] of its morphematic, syntactic and semantic systems etc.

That this is possible we know from the fact that some children learn to read "all by themselves", i.e. just by observing a text while listening to other people reading it.

In a talk given at the annual meeting of American reading specialists in Boston, in April 1968,[7] professor *Arthur I. Gates*, one of the foremost reading specialists in the United States, said that a recently finished investigation in the USA has shown that 80 % of the children beginning school in the USA can read a certain number of words. There are also facts revealed in this investigation that hint at the possibility that very soon children will learn to read exactly in the same way as they now learn to understand and express themselves in spoken language, i.e. by living a normally active and verbal life.

Now, if a child can learn to read at the same age and in the same way as he is learning to talk, the only prerequisite being that he be exposed to written language, how does he succeed in doing so?

The great debate about learning to read focused upon one big question: the acquisition of the code and the learning of the relationships between the letters of the written language and the sounds of the spoken language, the relations between graphemes and phonemes.

Even if we look at written language as an independent system, it is an undisputable fact that for a child with normal hearing the written language is inseparably connected with the spoken language. The written language is the counterpart if not the parallel of the spoken language. Summing up the investigations of his time, Edmund Burke Huey (1908) states (p. 117 f.) that there is no reading that is not accompanied by "inner speech" even if this inner speech is not combined with lip movements or other motor habits. The inner speech might just be an accompanying auditory impression of what is being read. The

---

[6] In fact Bloomfield and Fries come very near this proposition when they insist that phonics should not be taught explicitly but that the child should find out by himself. The difference is that Fries and Bloomfield use *adapted* material to attain this end.

[7] Published by *Landsforeningen af læsepædagoger*, Denmark, on the occasion of The Second World Congress on Reading, Copenhagen 1—3 August 1968.

reason for this inner speech seems to me to be that, even if a child learns to read totally without formal instruction, he is acquiring the written language more or less through the medium of and accompanied by the spoken language. He hears somebody else read a written message, he discovers that there is a relation between what is spoken and the signs he can see with his eyes. He attacks the writing and finds out the system—not only of the written language; he also discovers the relationships between this and the spoken language. This is done on all levels: not only on the grapheme-phoneme level, but also on the morphematic, the syntactic and the semantic levels. He will discover that written language has a sign *c* that might correspond to a spoken [s] or [k]. If the languages are spoken and written Swedish, he will also find out that the suffix [ʃoːn] in [reparaʃoːn] corresponds to the written *-tion*, but in [averʃoːn] to the written *-sion*. He will also discover that there are certain words and constructions characteristic of only written language, that written *en radio av hög kvalitet* may correspond to spoken *en jättefin radio*, that the genitive of the written *husets tak* corresponds to a prepositional phrase in the spoken *taket på huset* etc.

There has been much debate about the definitions of reading ability, and especially the sponsors of the reading-for-meaning method have tended to put the stress not on word recognition and word analysis—which eventually leads to the acquisition of the code—but rather on interpretation, appreciation and application of what is read (Chall p. 13). Even so, however, we must admit that reading knowledge rests on knowledge of the code. If you do not know the code you cannot—in a purely technical sense—attack every new word irrespectively of whether you have ever seen that word written or printed before. This has very little to do with your understanding of the meaning of the word. You do not know the meaning of Kilimanjaro, but you can read it nevertheless—if you know the code.

The first step to find how a child can succeed in learning to read in the same way as he learns to talk, i.e. by being exposed to written language, is therefore to find out how, under these circumstances, the code is acquired. To find out this is the aim of the following study.

Even if acquisition of the morphematic, syntactic and semantic systems of the written language is not the object of direct investigation here, it cannot be completely left out of the study. As should be seen in the following, morphemics, syntactics and semantics are implied in the code aspect also. In language graphemics-phonemics, morphemics, syntactics and semantics are interwoven and interdependent, you cannot study one without paying attention to the other. In "Reading: A Linguistic Perspective" (1969) Ronald Wardhaugh, summing up his views in a definition of reading, says: "When a person reads a text, he is attempting to discover the meaning of what he is reading by using the visual clues of spelling, his knowledge of probabilities of occurrence, his contextual-pragmatic knowledge, and his syntactic and semantic competence to give a meaningful interpretation to the text. Reading is not a passive process, in which a reader takes something out of the text without any effort or merely recognizes what is in the text. Nor does it appear to be a process in which he first recognizes what is on the page and then interprets it, a process in which a stage of decoding precedes a stage of involvement with meaning ... Reading is instead an active process, in which the reader must make an active contribution by drawing upon and using concurrently various abilities that he has acquired" (p. 133).

Chapter Two
The aim of this treatise. Method used in the experiment

The basis for this treatise is the assumption that a child can learn to read at the same age and in the same way that he learns to speak. The aim of the treatise is to find out how this learning is accomplished, particularly how the code is acquired.

The problem is then to find a method of exposing a child to written language in the same way as he is exposed to spoken language, in order to be able to make the necessary observations.

Because of the nature of written language this is almost impossible. A child learns to talk simply because everybody is talking around him and to him. He is constantly exposed to talk, talk that to a great extent deals with things and happenings about him and familiar to him, talk with a reference to things here and now and with a bearing on his present situation. Moreover, in talk there is mutual communication, the child being talked to may take an active part in the conversation, verbally or otherwise, thus showing his reactions and forcing the speaker to suit his mode of speaking to the child's mental capacity.

To be able to expose a child to written language in the same way, we should be forced to change our society into a writing society, communicating solely by pen and paper. This reminds us of the fact that in normal human communication written language is always a secondary language.

Moreover the written material surrounding the child is not "child-centered". Books and newpapers have no bearing on the actual situation of the small child. Both their contents and their language are often far beyond a child's capacity and interests. Exceptions are simple advertisements with a picture and one or two words (like "Drink Coca-Cola"), inscriptions on signboards etc. and some picture books for children.

To expose the child to written material in exactly the same way as he is exposed to spoken language is thus not feasible. Another and more serious point, however, is the following. Our study should concern itself particularly with the question how the code is acquired. Now, how are you able to observe and follow the acquisition of the code? The child must in some way communicate his learning process to the investigator and this must be done through the spoken language; that is, the child must read aloud.

We therefore choose to expose the child to the written language through the medium of the spoken language but try to do this in a way that implies an absolute minimum of instruction.

One method of presenting reading material to a child with a minimum of instruction is the way described by Glenn Doman in his book *How to Teach your Baby to Read* (1964). After having studied Doman's book in 1965 I found his method almost completely devoid of formal instruction. Moreover, the children supposed to learn through Doman's method ideally should be two years old, i.e. they are then exactly in the middle of the period when, according to Lenneberg, the onset of speech should take place. In reading Doman's book I also realized that the way Doman presents written language to small children resembles to a certain extent the way children are confronted with spoken language.

For the benefit of the reader, I shall here give a short account of Doman's method, trying to analyse it and to state in what respects it might accord with or violate our principle of "free exposure" without inflicting any instruction on the child.

Words are written on cards, one word on each card. To begin with, the letters should be red and 12.5 cm high.[8] The cards are presented to the child at a maximum rate of one a day.

The first word is *mother*. When the child says "mother" as soon as you show that card, you go to the next card, which reads *father*. When you are sure that the child can discriminate the "mother" card from the "father" card you proceed to nouns denoting parts of the body (*hand, nose, ear* etc.). These words are written with 10 cm high red letters. Then you go on to what Doman calls the vocabulary of the home: words denoting the child's toys and other personal belongings, words denoting well-known things in the house etc. The child should be able to see and

---

[8] The letters should be red to attract the attention of the child and they should be big enough to make even a small child able to *perceive* the word. Doman makes a great point of this. In his opinion the reason why small children do not learn to read all by themselves at a very early age is that the letters of printed matter are generally not big enough.

touch the thing at the same time as the "teacher" pronounces the word and shows the card to him.[9]

The domestic vocabulary also includes some verbs denoting simple actions well known to the child. The teacher may, to begin with, illustrate a verb by performing the action at the same time as he pronounces the corresponding word and shows the card. The domestic vocabulary should be written down in red letters 7.5 cm high.

All the time the "teacher" should be careful not to go on presenting new words without making sure that the child recognizes the old ones.

Then a book is provided. It should be a very simple and short book, not containing more than 150 different words. The letters should be 3/4 cm high.

The "teacher" copies the book, rewriting it in black letters 2.5 cm high. Then each word is written on a card, in 5 cm high black letters. These cards are presented to the child one by one in the same way as before.

When the child knows all the words, the words are put together to form the sentences of the book. The cards are put on the floor side by side, and the child now learns to read sentences, one sentence a day. When the child can read all the sentences of the book in this way he is given the handwritten copy of the book and is taught to read the sentences from this copy: reading left to right, from the top of the page to the bottom of the page.

When the child is well familiar with this handwritten copy, the printed book is presented to him. And now he will be able to read this fluently, in spite of the fact that the letters are only 3/4 cm high.[10]

You go on with other books, and now it is not necessary to have an intermediate handwritten copy. All words new to the child are written down on cards and shown to him. When the child knows these words he gets the new book etc.

After the child has read one or two books, you write down the alphabet small letters and capitals, each letter on one card. You present the cards to the child, telling him the names of the letters like this: about *a* "This is a small 'ei' ", about *A* "This is a capital 'ei' ", etc.

It is to be observed that the child is not taught the sound values of the letters but is just given the conventional names—with the qualifier

---

[9] In this way one makes sure not only that a strong association is established between the written and the spoken form but also that meaning is attached immedately to the written form; see above p. 5 f.

[10] Note the successive adaptation to smaller and smaller letters.

"small" and "capital" included in the name of the letter. This is obviously done to help the child to discern the letters within the word units. Contrary to C. C. Fries, however, you do not help the child to discern the *distinctive features* of the letters; you just present the letters to the child and let him find out by himself.

The words of the book are presented to the child without any kind of instruction. C. C. Fries also recommends the learning of words, but he makes a careful selection and ordering of words presented according to *spelling patterns:* "It is in *this selection and ordering of the material to be put into these exercises, not only for the first steps but for the complete process of the entire 'transfer stage'* that modern linguistic knowledge can make one of its chief contributions to the teaching of reading" (Fries, p. 199).[11]

By presenting the letters you no doubt draw the child's attention to the code. But as one avoids any kind of sounding and instead obscures what associations there might occur between letter and sound by adding the qualifier "small" and "capital" to the conventional name of the letter, this presentation cannot be said to help the child to discover the relations between letters and sounds.[12] Nor, as the letters are presented in their alphabetic order without being grouped according to distinctive features, do you give any hints about the graphematic system; instead the child is left to make the discoveries totally on its own.

The way of presenting the letters of the alphabet to the child in order to help him to discern the letters within the word units might be compared with what most adults do when they hear that a child who has begun to talk does not master a particular sound: they pronounce the sound separately and ask the child to do the same.

Apart from this teaching of the alphabet, Doman makes certain other adaptations of the written material:
1. the letters are bigger than is normal;
2. the child is first presented to nouns and verbs;
3. the words are concrete and they are illustrated so as to make sure the meaning is understood.

In my opinion these adaptations are very much like the adaptations made in talking to small children:
1. you often talk to a small child learning to speak in a distinct and clear voice;
2. you talk to a baby in very short sentences, often repeating, or at least

---

[11] It is to be observed that Fries uses the word *exercises*. The Doman method contains no exercises at all.
[12] Cf. though p. 83 and p. 85 note 70a.

putting heavy stress on, particular nouns or verbs that carry the essential meaning of what you want to say; moreover the first sentences
of the baby are one-word sentences, often consisting of one noun or
one verb;

3. when a child first learns a word in speech it is in a concrete situation
where the denoted thing is present. You never talk to babies about
abstractions.

Whatever other adaptations may be made, such as choosing simple
books with a simple language, they are in accordance with our principle to introduce the child to the written language through the medium
of the spoken language. It goes without saying that this means that the
written language presented to the child must be founded on the child's
own knowledge of the spoken language. Our only way of knowing any-
thing about this knowledge is to listen to the child. Thus, if the child
talks in only three to five-word sentences one should be careful not to
choose books where the sentences are much longer or more complicated
than that.[13]

The real instruction given is purely technical and non-linguistic.
The child is taught to read from left to right and from the top of the page
to the bottom. The child is taught to turn the pages right-left.

By using the Doman method you *leave it to the child* to find out the in-
terrelations between the codes of the written language and the spoken
language all by himself.

The Doman method is, then, a way of presenting written material to
a child *with a minimum of instruction and through the medium of the spoken
language*.

Using the Doman method it is therefore possible to make observations
about how a child discovers the correspondences between letters
and sounds, how he succeeds in interrelating the graphematic and the
phonematic systems—in "breaking the code"—which is the necessary
prerequisite if he is to attain full reading ability.

In carrying out this investigation I have studied only one child. My
aim has been to make a close and detailed study to find out certain elementary facts about the reading process.[14] Such a deep single study
will enable us to build up a description that can later be used and tested
by extending the investigation to wider material.[15] It is my opinion that

[13] In this respect Fries is of the same opinion (see Fries p. 202).
[14] I strongly stress the fact that this paper is not intended to test the usefulness of
the Doman method.
[15] See Chapter Eleven, *Suggestions for further investigation.*

both kinds of investigation are necessary: the close clinical study and the statistical one. But the close study should come first; before having made a close observation of a single case we do not know what questions are relevant when making an investigation on a big scale.[16]

[16] Also among psychologists this opinion seems to have gained ground. At the Second World Congress on Reading, in August 1968, Ruth Stranger and Arthur I. Gates both stressed the need for "close clinical studies".

Chapter Three
The experiment

The experiment started at the end of September, 1965. A girl, aged two years and four months, was taught to read Swedish by the method described on pp. 12—15.

During the first six weeks the child was presented with words denoting things and actions familiar to her. The cards were shown to her in bed before she went to sleep in the evening. She never got more than one new word a day, and before looking at the new card for the day we always went through the old ones to make sure that she recognized them. All the time the "teaching" consisted only of: 1. showing new cards to the child and telling her what was written on these cards; 2. showing old cards and asking what was written on them.

In the middle of November the words of a book were written down on cards. Now she soon began to ask for more than one new card a day, and in December she sometimes got up to three or four new cards a day. I took care never to give her as many cards as she really wanted to have and also not to make the sessions too long.

The child was able to read her first book on the 22nd of December 1965, i.e. when the experiment had been going on for three months. The cards belonging to that book were then set aside, and the words of a new book were codified on cards and presented in the same way as before. Thus the first session with the material from the new book began by showing the girl the first new card related to this book and telling her what was written on it. At the next session this first card was shown to her and she was asked to read it; then the second card was presented to her, etc.[17] To avoid tiring repetition very short books were chosen.[18]

When we had gone through the words of the second book, she got the book to read. After she had read it through once aloud—this reading took several sessions—the book was placed on her own book-shelf and she was allowed to read it and play with it as she pleased. Then the

---

[17] She was always allowed to take the new card in her hand and have a real look at it.
[18] Cards from an old book were shown only as far as words from that book returned in a new book.

third book was codified and presented in the same way as the second one.

During the sessions I took notes of what the girl said about the cards and about reading in general.

At the beginning of March, 1966—after five months of reading—the girl began making spontaneous efforts to read the new cards by herself, i.e. when I showed a new card to her she "read" the card before I had time to tell her what was written on it.[19] These attempts at reading were noted down.[20]

In April 1966 the spontaneous readings had become so frequent that I changed the method of showing new cards. Instead of taking a new card and saying "This reads X" I took the new card, showed it to her and asked "What does this read?" Every attempt at reading was carefully noted down.

During this active period the child's capacity for learning new words greatly increased. In April she got about five new words a day, in July about ten.[21]

During three weeks in August (9th—31st) there was no reading at all because of my holidays. On September 1st the experiment was continued in the same way as before by asking the child to read the new words, taking down what she said, and finally giving the right reading in cases where she did not succeed in reading a new word correctly.

At the beginning of November 1966 the child was able to read almost any new word[22] presented to her on a card. The "transfer stage", to use Fries's term, had been passed.

From the beginning of December 1966 the child was given new books directly, without the intermediate stage of showing cards. The girl read the books aloud to me and I took notes. Tape recordings of spontaneous reading of texts not prepared beforehand were also taken at intervals, but these have been of only little interest for this study.

In the following account of facts revealed during the experiment I have made a division into periods:

1. First period (September 30th 1965—December 22nd 1965; age 2 years,

---

[19] To stimulate her attempts I made a pause after showing her a new card, never telling her immediately what was written on it.

[20] Often the girl made many successive attempts. If all these attempts were unsuccessful, she was finally told the right reading.

[21] All at her own request, although I took great care always to give her many less than she really wanted to have.

[22] It goes without saying that she was only given words from books corresponding to her mental capacity. Cf. Fries p. 202.

4 months—2 years, 7 months): From the first word to the first book. (Chapter IV.)

2. Second period (December 23rd 1965—March 31st 1966; age 2 years, 7 months—2 years, 10 months): Including the first attempts at spontaneous reading of new words. (Chapter V.)

3. Third period (April 1st 1966—beginning of November 1966; age 2 years, 10 months—3 years, 5 months): The gradual development from haphazard attempts at reading new words to the ability to read any new word. (Chapters VI, VII and VIII.)

The description and discussion of these three periods form the central part of this treatise.

A special chapter (IX) has been devoted to capital letters, double syngraphemes and some grapho-phonematic irregularities, some of which were not mastered until the autumn of 1967.

A few words should be said here about the collection of data. Why have I not made tape recordings of all the sessions but used the more conventional method of taking notes?

The primary reason is that I wanted to make the sessions as natural as possible, both for the child and for myself. The girl was always to feel that we were playing together. Often we talked about other things in between; the girl invented games with the cards and I let her take her time. This relaxed atmosphere would have been extremely hard to maintain with a tape recorder on all the time. Besides, a child very soon discovers about the use of a recorder, and then the interest would have been centered on the recording and her own role there instead of on books and reading.[23]

But also from the point of view of linguistic analysis notes seemed preferable in this experiment. When taking notes I always give the non-linguistic data necessary in order to understand the notes when I analyse them later on. When using a tape recorder, however, I very easily trust this machine too much, forgetting that it cannot do all the job. Analysing the recording afterwards therefore becomes a very hard job. It would thus have been necessary for me to write down, to record and at the same

---

[23] My misgivings in this respect seem to have been well founded. I made some tape recordings of her reading from books, and after one of these sessions she said rather self-confidently "Don't you think I read well?" I then let her listen to her own voice and pointed out some mistakes, upon which she looked rather disappointed. —Somebody might say that my taking notes would arouse the child's curiosity as much as recording. But she was used to seeing me taking notes, so it didn't—not until she read so well that she was able to read my handwriting.

time to lead the experiment in such a way that the child had the impression that we were playing together.[24] Moreover, for the purpose of this investigation it turned out to be quite enough to use a very broad transcription, a sort of modified spelling, when writing down the girl's readings. I therefore decided to leave the recorder alone when she was reading cards and only use it now and then to record reading from books.

In order not to damage the experiment I had to see to it that there was no outside interference. Nobody else was allowed to instruct the girl or to teach her new words. Nor was the girl allowed to read new books herself outside the experiment.[25] But books already read were freely at her disposal, and I daresay she took advantage of the opportunity offered.

[24] A technical assistant would not have solved the problem.
[25] This is a rather important point. To be able to analyse her attempted readings I had to rely on such words as she had already learnt and try to explain the new attempts as analogies etc. But then I had to make sure that I really knew all the patterns. See p. 29 ff.

Chapter Four
First period (Sep. 30th 1965—Dec. 22nd 1965): From the first word to the first book

From the first day the girl was very enthusiastic about the reading cards with big, red letters on them. A characteristic thing about children between two and three seems to be their great receptivity. There were no difficulties whatever during the first six weeks, when she was presented only with concrete nouns and verbs. To her the written words were the things, and the cards with *mormor* (grandmother), *morfar* (grandfather), *kudde* (pillow) etc. immediately became favourites.

From the seventh week of reading, when the words were taken from books, she sometimes was shown words with unpleasant associations. These were met with disgust: "Mamma, jag blir så rädd när det står *hemskt* på en läslapp" (Mother, I get so frightened when it says *frightful* on a reading card).[26]

In the seventh week of reading I shifted over to a book and wrote down the words from it on cards, this time with black letters. Although she made her objections to the letters being black, this fact did not disturb her learning. But another and more serious problem arose. The first lines of the book read like this:

Lasse, sa Pelle. Vet du *vad*   (Lasse, Pelle said. Do you know
det är för dag *i* dag?   what day it is today?
Ja, sa Lasse. *I* dag   Yes, Lasse said. Today
är det i dag.   is today.)

The first five words afforded no problem, but *vad* (what) and the other words italicized above were met with less enthusiasm.

From the point of view of semantic content our vocabulary might be divided roughly into two groups:

1. words with a *heavy semantic load* such as nouns, adjectives and main verbs;
2. words carrying a *small semantic load* such as conjunctions, prepositions, some adverbs and pronouns, auxiliaries etc.

[26] The red cards were in fact considered unique. As an experiment I wrote one of the well-known "red" words with black letters on a new card and showed it to her. She looked very surprised: "Are there *two* of them?"

Words belonging to the first group function as subject, predicate and object in the sentence, that is, they carry the essential part of information. These words are sometimes called *contentives* as they carry information, i.e. semantic *content*. Words of the second group link the parts of the sentence together or express simple semantic relations. These might be called *functors* as their grammatical functions are more obvious than their semantic content.[27]

The contentives normally have heavy stress; the functors have weak stress or are unstressed.

In their paper *Three Processes in the Child's Acquisition of Syntax*[27] Roger Brown and Ursula Bellugi have shown that when learning to speak children first talk in contentives, and that they learn to use functors much later. The authors connect this with several facts, among them the "abstract" character of the functors and their weak stress.

Now, returning to our passage quoted above from the girl's first book, the five crucial words in italics there are functors. The girl herself gave an explanation why she disliked one of these words, the word "what": "När vi läser *tunga* gör vi så här" (When we read tongue we do like this)—she puts out her tongue[28]—"men *vad?*" (but *what?*)

The reason why the girl objected to the functors must have been their lack of reference, their small semantic load or "abstractness" as compared with the words learnt earlier. Another important fact is that functors very seldom occur alone. This is true both of spoken and written language. Thus, in presenting to the child a single functor written down on a card, you construct a *non-linguistic situation.*[29]

On very special occasions, however, functors may be used alone—as in headings, glossaries etc. and as used metalinguistically, i.e. when you *talk about* the word "vad"—and in these cases they have a special pronunciation called *lexical pronunciation.* In presenting a card with a functor to the child you always use this lexical pronunciation, a

[27] See Roger Brown and Ursula Bellugi, *Three Processes in the Child's Acquisition of Syntax* (New Directions in the Study of Language. Ed. Eric H. Lenneberg. MIT Press 1964).

[28] When reading the earliest words we often illustrated them, that is gave the reference, thus affording a more natural linguistic situation.

[29] Adults seem to react in the same way towards isolated functors. In a reading experiment with adults at the beginning of this century *Edmund Burke Huey* presented isolated words on squares of cardboard. The connective and relational words did not then suggest any imagery to the readers. "Because of this absence of imagery the exposure of these words was regarded with much displeasure, their isolated appearance seeming to be regarded as anomalous" (p. 154).

pronunciation that is totally unknown to the child and which does not help him to tie the form to the corresponding spoken functor as used in context.[30]

So I decided to give up the book with too many functors and to write a special book myself, taking care: 1. that there were as few functors as possible; 2. that the sentences were short; 3. that the vocabulary was suited to a child of two and a half, and 4. that the story appealed to her.

This adaptation of the material does not interfere with the experiment. It is not an adaptation made to draw the child's attention to certain correspondences between written and spoken language or to teach the structure of written language. The adaptations made simply correspond to those you might make in talking to a small child when you take pains both to hold its attention and to make yourself understood: you talk distinctly, in a simple and concrete vocabulary, using only short sentences[31] and choosing a topic that interests your listener (see p. 14 f).

Then the words of this home-made book were learnt. The few functors there were—like *i* (in)—continued to arouse difficulties because the girl did not want to pay any attention to them. Then I made another adaptation. To eliminate the constructed non-linguistic situation where functors are learnt out of context, I decided to present the functors first on separate cards and immediately afterwards put them on the floor together with well-known words *forming a sentence*.[32] Thus I began to form sentences before all the words of the first book had been learnt. But to avoid combining the first sentence-reading with the already unpopular functors, thus linking disagreeable associations with sentence-reading as such, I first made sentences out of concrete words, like *Mormor äter fisk* (Grandmother eats fish).

The reading of sentences was received with great applause, and when I then began putting functors into the sentences, they did not cause any more trouble.

---

[30] If the child understands and uses this functor in his own speech. As Brown and Bellugi point out children generally do not master all the major varieties of simple English sentences until they are 36 months old. The girl in this experiment was 30 months when she met her first functor in written language.

[31] The connection between sentence-length and the age of the child has been frequently observed, see for instance McCarthy (1954).

[32] Such an adaptation, although it is of a linguistic kind, should not interfere with the experiment. On the contrary it is a modification of the Doman method making the learning situation more like the situation in which children learn to talk, where they are always exposed to *genuine spoken language:* i.e. you expose the child to *genuine written language*, not to parts of written language that do not occur isolatedly.

When the words of the book were learnt the cards were put on the floor to form the sentences of the book. There is nothing special to note about that stage of the experiment. When all the sentences had been produced and read—about one sentence a day—the book was shown to the girl. Now something curious happened. When presented with a whole page full of wonderful words the girl did not read horizontally and from left to right all the time; instead she skipped and jumped in all directions.

The Western convention of reading horizontally, from left to right, was very soon established, however—it was made much easier by the fact that the girl had already read the sentences many times on the floor and knew the order of the words in these sentences beforehand.

During the first three months of reading the child learnt to recognize some 120 words, about 40 "red-letter words" and 80 from the first book. Now, returning to the theory that a child is able not only to memorize but also to analyse and classify linguistic material thus finally discovering the system—were there any signs already at this initial stage of such analysis and classification?

At the end of the first month of reading the girl made her first comment on the reading material, showing she was beginning to analyse words: "Mamma, *mage* liknar *öga*" (Mother *mage* (stomach) is like *öga* (eye)). The letter *g* seems to have attracted her attention. The *g* no doubt is the most special in character of the letters in the two words, perhaps also the most dominant.[33]

In the third month of reading the girl learnt the word *precis*. She then observed: "*precis* liknar *pappa*" (*precis* is like *pappa*)—pointing at the *p* in *precis*—"men i *pappa* e de tre stycken" (but in *pappa* there are three of them).

This shows three things: 1. she was able to discern the letter *p* in *precis* and looked on it as an entity;[34] 2. she was able to identify and

---

[33] In 1900 J. Zeitler showed that dominant letters are recognized more correctly (J. Zeitler, *Tachistoskopische Untersuchungen über das Lesen*). Quoting Zeitler, Huey says: "In general, 'the more characteristically' a letter is shaped, the more clearly is it recognized." (Huey, p. 83).

[34] It is to be observed that one of the first letters recognized is *p*. O. Kutzner in *Kritische und experimentelle Beiträge zur Psychologie des Lesens mit besonderer Berücksichtigung des Problems der Gestaltqualität* (1916) has shown that ascenders and descenders are recognizing cues.—Moreover the *p*'s in *precis* and *pappa* are situated in the beginning of the word, in *pappa* also in the middle of the word; compare C. F. Wiegand, *Untersuchungen über die Bedeutung der Gestaltqualität für die Erkennung von Wörtern (Zeitschrift für Psychologie und Physiologie der Sinnesorgane*, 1907).

sum up three samples of the same entity; 3. she had a visual image of the word *pappa* that was strong enough to enable her to pick out the three *p*'s from it.

The visual image of the word *pappa* must have been very clear. This does not imply, however, that all the other words the girl was able to recognize were necessarily as clear in her visual memory. *Pappa* belonged to the early words; it does contain only two different kinds of letters; it is symmetrically built up with the double *p* surrounded by *a*'s on each side, and it appealed to the girl's emotions.[35]

Nevertheless her observations on *precis* and *pappa* give us a cue to the process behind the acquisition of reading ability: words are learnt visually and stored. As soon as a new word is introduced, this word is not only "put into the bag" but it is analysed and compared with the visual images of the words learnt before. By means of such comparisons structure is discovered.

In the reading material from the first book there were only two words causing any difficulties: *när* (when) and *där* (there) were confused. The cause of the trouble seems to have been twofold: 1. the two words are functors; 2. from the point of view of spelling *när* and *där* form a minimal pair. When repeating the reading cards of the book I therefore chose to present the two words *när* and *där* to the girl first one after the other, then both simultaneously. This way of showing the two similar words was taken up by the girl herself when she next met with a functor, the word *det*. She then made the following comment: "*det* liknar *dem*, ta fram *dem* så får vi likna" (*det* is like *dem*, show *dem* to me and let us compare).[36] Like the observations on *precis* and *pappa* this shows that new words are analysed and *compared* with the visual images of words learnt earlier.

The observations made during the first three months of the experiment might briefly be summed up as follows:

1. Insofar as the words written down on cards denoted persons or things well known to the child, she treated these cards as if they had been these persons or things.[37]

2. Functors were difficult to learn out of context.

[35] Compare what has been said above about favourite words.

[36] The trouble with the girl's remarks (here and elsewhere in this book) is that rendered in English translations they sound too adult-like. In fact she was using the childish language typical of her age with many new formations that are not possible to translate. In this example she did not use the normal Swedish equivalent to *compare* but instead a verb formed on the Swedish adjective *lik* (Eng. *like*). This verb, *likna*, normally means "resemble".

[37] See S. I. Hayakawa, *Language in Thought and Action* (London 1959) p. 29.

3. Similarities between word images were noticed by the child (*mage—öga*).
4. Certain letters were distinguished (*precis — pappa*).
5. When the child learnt words, she acquired visual images of those words. As she was introduced to new words she compared them with the images of old words, and similarities and differences were noticed.

Chapter Five
Second period (Dec. 23rd 1965—March 31st 1966): The first attempts at spontaneous reading of new words

During the fourth and fifth months of reading (Dec. 23rd 1965—February 28th 1966) four new books were gone through. These books contained in all about 150 words that were new to the girl.

Only a few of the new words were functors. One new functor was *ner* (down). When I showed it to the girl she remarked: "Precis som 'ta ner skynket' " (As in 'ta ner skynket'), i.e. she put the word into a context to make sure that she knew the meaning.[38]

Now the girl was also shown the individual letters (see above p. 13). This knowledge of the names of letters does not seem to have had any direct effect on her progress in reading, though indirectly it might have had such an effect. Knowing the names of the letters, she now was able not only to say "*m*ed is like *m*other" but also "*m*ed has a small *m* like *m*other". Her eagerness to make comparisons seemed to increase with her new ability to make more exact statements about similarities and dissimilarities between words. This might in turn have had a stimulating effect on her discrimination between different words and her learning of new words.

The comparisons made during this period almost always referred to *initial* letters. The child somehow seemed to look upon the initial letter as the "face" of the word. This is evident from the following incident. The girl had just learnt the letter *D*. Her reading vocabulary also contained the word *Dumbom* written with a capital initial letter. One day when I took the alphabetic cards she caught sight of the card with the letter *D* on it and said: "Mamma, du skall ge mig Dumboms fotografi" (Mother, give me the photo of Dumbom).

A small initial letter was also called the "photo" of the word. On the 16th of February the girl read the word *ned* for the first time,

---

[38] In the above-mentioned experiment by Huey (note 29), the readers confronted with isolated functors got "few associations of any kind except verbal ones, usually phrases of which they constantly form a part" (Huey, p. 154).

and on the following day she asked me to bring her *ned* (down) and *med* (with). She then put the two cards beside each other and said: "De e samma" (That is the same)—pointing at the two *d*'s—"å de e samma" (and that is the same)—pointing at the two *e*'s—"men den (*med*) har mammans fotografi, å de har inte den (*ned*)" (but that one (*med*) has mother's photo and that one (*ned*) hasn't).[39]

This last example also shows us that analyses and comparisons might go on for a long time after the moment of learning. The new word *ned* had been shown to the girl early one evening, and the comments on *ned* and *med* were on the following morning.

So far we have treated almost solely the formal or technical side of reading, the child's reactions to words and letters as graphic entities. But what about the semantic side? Did the child understand what she was reading? Did she ever make any comments on the contents of the books?

On the 22nd of December she read her first book—the home-made one. The book was then put into her own bookcase and she treated it as a favourite toy, returning to it several times a day, reading it over and over to herself, again and again. The book was about her cousin Anna and herself and their families. One passage told about how Anna was pushing her dolls in a pram. Having read this passage the girl asked me one day to give her the reading card with *pram* on it. She took this card in her hand, looked up the passage about Anna and the pram in the book and said: "Now Anna is driving her pram and I am driving mine".

Another passage in the book related that her father would come and spend his Christmas holidays with us. Now, Father fell ill and was taken to hospital, so he could not come. The girl did not make any comment on this passage until two months after she had read the book for the first time. Then she suddenly said: "My big book is wrong when it says that Father came on that day he was in hospital. I am going to check it. When I become a big girl I am going to write all of it correctly".

The story about the pram shows that the experiencing of the contents must be very strong; one would almost be tempted to say that to the small child the word is the thing (compare above p. 21). The second example shows that the child was able to make the distinction between

[39] Referring to experiments made by Goldscheider and Miller, Huey (p. 80) says: "To the determining letter class belongs the first letter of a word, almost always".

reality and written representation of reality, but that she asked for absolute conformity between the two.

In March, which was the sixth month of reading, a new stage was reached as the girl then began to make her first attempts at *reading* the new cards presented to her before I told her what was written on them. Eleven attempts at reading were made, nine of which were successful.[40]

The new words that the girl tried to read were all made up of material from words learnt earlier, i.e. they might be: 1. parts of already learnt words 2. combinations of words and/or parts of words learnt before.

The method of putting all the words of the books on reading cards gave me a complete index to the child's reading vocabulary. This enabled me to find very easily the patterns for every attempted independent reading of a new word.

According to how the girl made use of already learnt material when trying to read new words, the attempted readings could be divided into three groups, here called *adjunctions, deletions* and *substitutions*.

Adjunctions. On the 1st of March the girl was shown the new word *bäcken* and read it correctly. Earlier she had learnt to read *bäck*. The rest of the word was also well known to her as she had already met *en* as an indefinite article eleven times in her first book. I assume the underlying process producing the correct reading *bäcken* to be as follows.

1. First *bäcken* is analysed into two parts, *bäck* and *en*. The child is able to make this analysis because she is well acquainted with these parts as written entities.
2. The two parts are then read together, forming a spoken entity that is well known to the child and immediately associated with a meaning.
3. Thus the new graphic entity *bäcken* is tied to the corresponding spoken entity and is associated with the same meaning, all without the interference of the teacher.

Putting the stress on the second step in the process, which is the adding up of already known entities, we call this reading *adjunction*.

Correct adjunctions of the same kind, made in March, are *jadå* March 24th (*ja+då*), *hattaffären, klockaffären, hundaffären* March 26th

---

[40] The remarkably high percentage of successful attempts merely shows that the girl was very cautious, trying to read a word by herself only when she felt absolutely sure that she was right, never guessing. As time went on she became much bolder, and in July the percentage of successful readings was only about 50, owing to the fact that she then tried to read almost all new words by herself.

(*hatt/klocka/hund* + *affären*). An incorrect adjunction is *lilla broren* (read as two words) instead of *lillebror* (previously learnt words: *lilla* and *bror*).

In the examples given above two parts already learned as separate graphic entities are put together. A more complicated kind of adjunction was made for the first time at the end of March when the new word *pengarna* was read correctly. Earlier the girl had learnt to read *pengar*. But the rest of the word, -*na*, does not occur as an isolated entity; it is a so-called bound morpheme, functioning as a definite article in the plural: pojkar*na*, flickor*na*, ballonger*na* etc. The adjunction here implies putting together one entity already learnt as a "word image" with another entity that is only a *part* of word images learnt before.

To be able to read *pengarna* the child must thus be able to recognize -*na* from previously learnt written words with this ending, i.e. she must already have made a grapho-morphemic analysis of these words.

At the moment of the independent correct reading of *pengarna* the girl had already met the following words ending in -*na*: *tassarna, kattungarna, fjärilarna, fåglarna, grodorna, insekterna, blommorna*. The question is now: How did she succeed in distinguishing -*na* as an entity?

Above we have shown that as soon as the girl learnt a new word, she compared this word with similar ones learnt earlier and tried to find out the differences between them. In two of the books read by the girl before she made the correct reading *pengar-na* she had met the word *kattungar*, which word appeared twice before she met *kattungarna* (compare above!). In the word pair kattungar—kattungar*na* the only difference is -*na*, and as soon as the child had found this out she had in fact made the grapho-morphemic analysis necessary to look at -*na* as an entity within the higher units *tassarna, kattungarna, fjärilarna* etc.[41]

Theoretically she would now be able to read any previously learnt word + *na*.

Another adjunction of this kind made in March was *snurrorna* (*snurror,* -*na*).

Deletions. On the 2nd of March the girl read the new word *ugglan*. Earlier she had learnt *ugglans*. To make such a reading the girl must be able to analyse *ugglans* into *ugglan* + *s*, an analysis made possible by pairs occurring earlier, such as Anna — Anna*s*, Astrid — Astrid*s*, Mirran — Mirran*s* etc. I assume the underlying process to be as follows: 1. *ugglan* calls up the mental image of *ugglans*, learnt earlier;

---

[41] Provided that she understood the linguistic forms *kattungar, kattungarna*.

2. *ugglan* is compared with *ugglans* and the difference is observed;
3. on the basis of pairs like *Anna — Annas* etc. -*s* has already been identified as a meaningful unit. This helps the reader to analyse *ugglans*
   into *ugglan* + *s* and to recognize the new word *ugglan* as *ugglan(s)*.

If we stress this last part of the process we might call the reading
deletion.

There is always a certain danger in assuming the nature of underlying
mental processes. In this case, however, some evidence could be got from
the girl herself.

After showing a new reading card to the girl, I always let her take it
in her hand in order that she might really get acquainted with it. This
turned out to be of great importance to the experiment, as she began
to play with the cards and to talk about them in a way that told me a great
deal about the reading process.

On the 4th of March she took *ofta,* put her hand on *a* saying: "Now
it is not *ofta,* it is *oft.*" On the 21st of March *finns* was in the same way
made into *finn*: "Nu står det inte *finns,* nu står det *finn*" (Now it is not
finns, it is *finn*). Two days later she put her hand on *ar* in *kostar* and read
kost. In these three examples the girl was identifying and deleting letters
and combinations of letters that very often occur as morphemes: -*a*,
-*s*, -*ar*. In the girl's reading vocabulary at the beginning of March we
find the following pairs:

snäll — snäll*a*   Anna   — Anna*s*   (fot)boll   — boll*ar*
min — min*a*   Astrid — Astrid*s*   (jul)klapp — klapp*ar*
sov — sov*a* etc. Mirran — Mirran*s* etc.

On the basis of these pairs it is possible for the girl to identify the morphemes -*a*, -*s* and -*ar* and then add them to or delete them from previously learnt words.

The playing with words and parts of words described above con-
firms that readings like *ugglan(s)* should be looked upon as deletions.
In one case the girl even made a deletion overtly. Being shown the word
läs she immediately said: "It is like *läsa*. Fetch *läsa* and show it to me!"
I showed *läsa* to her, and she made the deletion "*läsa — läs*". The difference between *ugglan(s)* and *läs(a)* is that in *ugglan(s)* the deletion is
made on basis of the remembered word image *ugglans,* and in *läs(a)*
the word *läsa* is itself present.

Substitutions.   On the 25th of March the girl was shown the word *hittade.* She read it as *hittde.* Although unsuccessful, this reading was the
earliest example of a third type of spontaneous reading on the basis of
material learnt earlier.

An already known word was *hittat*. The graphemic sequence *de* was well known as a separate word (she had not met it earlier as a bound morpheme in verbs because her books so far had been written in the present tense). The mental process is assumed to be as follows: When being shown *hittade* the girl remembers first *hittat* then *de*. She realizes that *hittade* is *hittat* minus something at the end plus *-de*, and she then deletes *-at* and adds *-de*, that is substitutes *-de* for *-at* getting the (incorrect) form *hittde*. This reading might thus be called a *substitution*.[42]

Adjunctions, deletions and substitutions are the result of an analysis of the presented words; we therefore choose to call these readings *analytical readings*.

So far the spontaneously read new words consisted of earlier words or endings from words learnt earlier. On the 28th of March I received the first evidence that the girl was able to recognize a formerly learnt graphic entity occurring in the middle of a new word. Looking at *färghandeln* she hid *färg* and *deln* with her hands saying: "You can make *han* out of *färghandeln*." This shows that the analysis of words into sections is not confined to the boundaries set up by the morphemes. The following incident gives further evidence that non-morphematic parts are observed: *nog* was shown to the girl (24.3)*; she told me to bring her *stjärnor*; she then pointed at *-nor* saying: "Här står *nor*. De e inte samma, *nog* och *nor*" (Here is *nor*; *nog* is not the same as *nor*).[43]

By the middle of March we had gone through the whole alphabet, and the girl was now able to recognize all the letters when they were shown to her separately. She also showed that she was able to analyse a written word into letters. On the 6th of March looking at *köpa* she said spontaneously: "k, ö, p, a . . . köpa", i.e. she "read" the word in two ways, first giving the separate letters, then reading the whole word as an entity. It was, however, to be many months before she grasped the connection between the separate letters and the whole word. She still seemed to be interested primarily in the initial letters. For example, she said: "*fram* har ett *f*, ett litet *f*" (fram has got an *f*, a small *f*).

During the month of March the girl seemed to solve the problem of

---

[42] About *hittde,* see also p. 65.

* Abbreviation of dates follows European style: the day precedes the month.

[43] Probably the identification was made easier by the fact that *-nor* is made up of *n+or*, where *-or* is a morpheme and *-n* homographic with the morpheme functioning as a definite article in the previously learnt *flicka-n, fru-n, mamma-n, pojke-n, åker-n*. Compare false strings, pp. 70—71.

identifying functors. When she met a new functor on a reading-card, i.e. out of context—and for that matter also a word that is not tied to a semantic content possible to visualize—she often put it into a linguistic context.

Ex. *fram*: Vi går *fram* (March 2nd)

gång: En *gång* så skulle du gå, till pappa (March 3rd)

stannar: Jag *stannar* inne (March 4th)

bort: När jag skulle äta middag så var jag *bort*skämd (March 26th)
This habit of relating new words to linguistic contexts shows us that already at such a relatively early stage the child is keenly aware of the semantic side of reading. To read is not only to recognize graphic shapes; to read is to be told something, to receive information.

Being shown a reading-card related to a new book implies being presented with a word out of context. The girl's principal task in this situation was to memorize the graphic shape associated with a certain sound sequence, which was in turn associated with a more or less clear semantic content derived from the several speech situations where she had earlier come across the word. When finally given the new book, the girl met this new word in a specific context.

We have already shown by many examples that the visual "images" of learnt words are somehow stored in the brain and that new words are compared with these images.[44] But I have also received evidence that the words learnt seem to be stored in the brain *in their specific* contexts, so that when given a certain word the girl might answer by rendering a sentence from one of her books where this word occurs. By mistake, twice in March I gave the girl a card with a word on it that she had already learnt. She then looked at me and said: "I have had that before", and then word by word she said the sentence where this very word had occurred for the first time.

Ex. *bara*: " 'Små kaniner *bara* äter och äter och äter.' "

fryser: " 'Jag *fryser* ju', Det var Karo som sa det i Totos bok"
(Karo said so in the book about Toto).

Of course the continuous rereading of the books (see p. 28) must be of great importance in this ability to memorize. But I have noticed the same phenomenon in my girl's spoken language. A single example might suffice to illustrate this. One Sunday we went to church together. As

[44] Probably the ability to recall word images is mainly the result of the reading of cards where every word image is learnt isolatedly and thus stands out very clearly, although the repeated rereading of books might do much to strengthen the memorized images.

we entered, the choir was singing and the organist was playing. My girl then asked why they were singing already. I said something like: "Dom bara *övar* sig" (They are just *practising*). Several weeks later we read in a book: "Vi ... dansade ett litet slag kring granen bara för att *öva* oss till kvällen". The girl's comment came very quickly: "*Öva* sig i å sjunga till orgeln i Kummelby kyrka" (*Practice* singing to the organ in the church of Kummelby).

The ability to remember written contexts seemed to be extraordinarily well developed. As evidence of this I might mention something that happened after one year and three months of reading (Dec. 21st, 1966). I had given the girl three sets of reading-cards to play with. The sets belonged to three different books:

1. "*Fias fjärilar*", finished Nov. 21st, 1966.
2. "*Byn som glömde att det var jul*", finished Nov. 28th, 1966.
3. "*Mats kommer till stan*", finished Dec. 12th, 1966.

The cards were all mixed up. I had left the girl alone for a moment. When I entered the room I found her sitting there talking to herself and putting the cards into three different heaps, those belonging to "*Fias fjärilar*" in one heap etc. As soon as she was unsure where to put a card, she stopped for a moment, said the context in which she had met the word; and then, remembering to what book this linguistic context (sentence or part of sentence) belonged, she put the card into the right heap.

I mention this not to suggest that the girl must be a wonderfully clever child. If she were I would not have told the story. I mention it because I am strongly convinced that *here we have got a cue to the extraordinary linguistic ability of every normal child*. With its capacity for memorizing, a child stores linguistic contexts with an ease that seems miraculous to an adult. These memorized contexts form a perpetually accumulating background for new linguistic experience. The child forms his picture of the structure of language, its grammar and dictionary, from this stock of contexts, and as the contexts accumulate the child's private grammar and vocabulary come closer and closer to the "complete structure" or the correct grammar and dictionary of the language he is learning.[45]

Early reading of good reading material adapted to the total state of the child (intellect, feelings, interests, background etc.) might thus be

---

[45] See above p. 7. — See also R. Söderbergh "*Strukturer och normer i barnspråk*".

of great importance to the linguistic and mental development of the child, as reading material permits repetition which greatly enhances the effect: you may go back and read a text over and over again if you wish to. And that is exactly what the child does and loves to do.

A similar effect is of course attained when patient adults read the same book or tell the same story over and over again at the child's request. But most parents no doubt can affirm that they very seldom have sufficient time and patience to satisfy their children in this respect. When the youngster reads by himself this is no longer any problem, and you need not frustrate your child by depriving him of the intellectual stimulus that is of such vital importance to him.

The remarkable need for linguistic repetition in early childhood disappears later on and so does the fabulous capacity for memorizing. My personal opinion is that the need for repetition has something to do with the learning process. The games of the young—both animals and children—are said to be a sort of practice towards attaining all the accomplishments needed later on in life. In the same way, linguistic repetition might be instinctive training carried on by the child in order to master the instrument that enables us to function as human beings cooperating in a complicated society and making use of the accumulating funds of knowledge: l a n g u a g e.

Before finishing this chapter a few words should be said about the technical progress in reading aloud that could be observed during the month of March.

When reading her first book the girl had been taught to point at the words. This was to accustom her to the left-to-right convention and to make sure that she did not skip any words.

On the 4th of March I noticed the girl sitting in a corner reading a book that she had finished a fortnight earlier. She read it whispering and without pointing. About three weeks later (March 23rd) she had just finished the reading-cards of another book and was going to read it aloud to me for the first time. She then read it without pointing. I did not make any comments to her about this, but I noticed that her reading now was much more like natural speech. When pointing she had been apt to make pauses between every word. After some minutes, however, she suddenly began to point, then interrupted herself: "No, it is much better not to point". "Much better" probably meant that she experienced reading without pointing as more meaningful. She was then able to take in bigger portions of the text at one time; her eyes could always be a good bit ahead of her voice and so the understanding of the text was better.[46] Evidence of better understanding was the fact that her intonation, stress and reading rhythm improved when she did not point.

[46] Edmund Burke Huey, summing up the results of research about the perceptual process in reading, at the beginning of this century wrote in *The Psychology and Pedagogy of Reading*: "In partial disregard, therefore, of the printer's divisions, there is naturally a gradual progress, with practice, towards recognition in larger units, for those who learn first the recognition of letters and words. Larger and larger unitary reactions are set off as familiarity makes this possible, the same excitations coming to serve as cues for the larger recognitions instead of for the smaller, while the earlier processes or recognition habits, even when they do not atrophy, are performed automatically, consciousness ever tending to leave them for higher levels" (p. 115); and "the reader's acquirement of ease and power in reading comes through increasing ability to read in larger units" (p. 116).

Chapter Six
Third period (April 1ˢᵗ 1966—Oct. 31ˢᵗ 1966): Introduction. The misidentifications

During the period from the beginning of April to the end of October the girl gradually acquired reading ability in the sense of being able to read almost any unknown word presented to her.

It is possible to follow the process behind this gradual acquisition by examining the girl's readings of all new words presented to her during the period and then comparing these new words and readings with words learnt earlier. Every attempted reading of a new word has something to do with already learnt words and might be described in terms of those words.

A. Misidentifications and analytical readings. An introductory comparison

Roughly speaking, the girl reacted in three ways to the new words presented to her. Sometimes she did not read them at all—this was often the case when the new words differed too much from words learnt before. If, however, there were enough similarities between the new words and earlier reading material, she chose one of two ways. Either she looked upon the new word as an entity, mistaking it for an already learnt word that had certain characteristics in common with the new word—as when *mugg* was taken to be *mun*, learnt earlier, or *sig* was read *sin*; such misreadings will here be called *misidentifications*—or, in comparing the new word with her "memory images" of already known words she made an analysis, finding out that the new word in some way must be made up of earlier words or parts of such words. In the last chapter we have already discussed such analytical readings, calling them *adjunctions*, *deletions* and *substitutions*.

The analytical readings may be right or wrong—right as when *bäcken* is read as a combination of the previously learnt entities *bäck* and *en*, wrong as when *julas* is assumed to be the sum of *jul* and *glass*. In both cases the reader has arrived at the result by adjunctions, but in the latter case one of the adjuncted parts has been misidentified.

Sometimes the reader might suggest different readings of the same word. Often she first tried the line of least resistance producing a misidentification, but on being told this reading was not correct she had another try, then either producing a new misidentification or using analytical reading.

A table of the number of presented words and words read during the period April—October 1966 looks as follows:

TABLE I. Number of words read

	April	May	June	July	September	October
Words presented	43	136	131	143	138	180
Words read	38	123	112	129	131	173
No reading	5(12 %)	13(9.5 %)	19(14.5 %)	14(9.7 %)	7(5 %)	7(3.8 %)

About 130—140 new words were presented each month except for April (43 words) and October (180 words). In April there was a break of 15 days around Easter when no supervised reading was done. The high number of words presented in October is due to the fact that at the end of that month the girl was given ten or more new words a day, as she had then "broken the code" and was able to read almost every new word presented to her. The figure of 180 thus indirectly reveals the higher degree of reading skill attained in October.

Increasing reading skill is also indicated by the line "No reading".[47] In April, 5 out of 43 words—that is 12 %—produced no reading. Before the summer holidays in August the percentage of words producing no reading never fell below 9.5 %. In September, however, only 5 % of the new words met with silence, and in October the corresponding number was as low as 3.8 %.[48]

TABLE II. Number of readings compared with number of words read

	April	May	June	July	Sept.	Oct.
Words read	38	123	112	129	131	173
Number of readings	40	142	115	141	153	175

[47] "No reading" means that on being presented with a new word the girl did not suggest any reading whatever, but I had simply to tell her what was written on the card.
[48] The high percentage in June—14.5 %—is probably due to the fact that in that month she was given books with a richer and more varied vocabulary. Thus the new words presented were not so often mere variations of old stems.

In this table the numbers of readings are accounted for. "One reading" means either that only one reading has been suggested for a new word or that two or several readings are tried, but that the later ones are only to be considered as adaptations of the first suggestion, i.e. the girl reveals her reading process by "thinking aloud" (compare synthesis, p. 94 f.).

We have two or more readings when several suggestions have nothing whatever in common but are just new disconnected tries.

From the table we see that in April, June and October the girl tries only about one reading for every word presented. In between, however, she is bolder and seems more keen on trying different ways of tackling a word. This tendency seems to culminate in September, the month before the code is broken.

The few readings in April are probably due to uncertainty—at that period she was not willing to try a reading if she was not compartively sure to be right. The decrease in number of readings in June is due to the fact that more difficult reading material was introduced—compare note 48. In October, however, the reason why every word is read only once seems to be that a new reading habit has been established: a new and difficult word is now usually read by breaking it up into small units, preferably graphemes (compare graphematic readings, p. 97). If she fails by this method, no other way of tackling the word is tried.

TABLE III. Number of correct readings

April	May	June	July	Sept.	Oct.
17 (43 %)	56 (39 %)	55 (48 %)	55 (39 %)	72 (47 %)	122 (70 %)

This table shows the percentage of correct readings. In April 43 % of the readings are correct. During the following months the percentage of correct readings fluctuates between 39 % and 48 %, and no significant increase is made until October, the month when the code is broken and when 70 % of the readings are correct.

Note that the fluctuations in the percentage of correctly read words in April—July follow the fluctuations in the "no reading" column (table I). In April and June the percentage of words not read is rather high— the reader is more careful when coming across difficult words. Accordingly the percentage of correct readings becomes comparatively high. In May and July, however, the reader is bolder; the percentage of no-readings is low and so is the percentage of correct readings. But in September and October this relation is reversed. The percentage of words not read is constantly sinking, but the number of correct readings is increasing—the stage of full reading ability is gradually being attained.

TABLE IV. Types of readings

	April	May	June	July	Sept.	Oct.
Misidentifications	8	30	21	21	32	9
Analytical readings	31	100	90	108	115	164
Unidentifiable	1	12	4	12	6	2

This table provides a classification of all the readings tried during the period. First the so-called misidentifications are listed, then we see all readings which may with certainty be described in terms of adjunctions, deletions or substitutions of material learnt earlier, and finally we see such readings as cannot with any amount of certainty be listed as either misidentifications or analytical readings.

It is significant that the proportion of misidentifications—where the new words are treated as entities—to analytical readings remains constant, the analytical readings being 3.5 to 5 times as common as the misidentifications, *until the month of October when the code is broken.* Then the analytical readings become 18 times more numerous than the misidentifications.

The reason for this change is that in October when the code is broken —i.e. when the girl suddenly understands completely the correspondence between grapheme and phoneme—she begins to use a quite new analytical technique when trying to read new words that cannot be read by means of adjunctions etc. of previously learnt words or morphemes: she "sounds" the words letter by letter. Earlier, on being asked to read a word that resisted the operations of adjunction etc. she had often just suggested a word learnt previously that looked similar, i.e. made a "misidentification". At the time when, as soon as a difficult new word is attacked, the analytical-synthetical process of identifying graphemes, sounding them and adding the sounds replaces the mere "looking", we may safely presume that full reading ability is being attained.

Thus the increase in the analytical readings as compared with the misidentifications indicates that in October the girl is reaching the stage of full reading ability.

B. The misidentifications. An analysis

From what has been said earlier it might be concluded that the misidentifications are the result of an inferior kind of reading in which a new word is carelessly observed, without any kind of analysis, and mistaken for one learnt earlier. This is not true, however. Some of the misidentifications are the result of chance readings, but as a rule they are the outcome of most careful considerations.

An investigation of the misidentifications shows that certain rather constant relations, as to *length, letters and position of letters,* exist between a new word given and the word it is wrongly supposed to be.[49]

Length of a new word given as compared with the word it is wrongly supposed to be. A new word, *såg,* might be mistaken for the previously learnt *stå;* in this case the word given and the word assumed have the same length. If, however, the new word *allihop* is assumed to be the previously learnt *Hoppelihopp,* it will be noted that there is a considerable difference in length between the two.

The correlation of length between a new word and the word it is assumed to be is shown by the following table:

TABLE V.

Length of words given in letters	Length of words assumed compared with words given										
	=	± 1	± 2		± 3		± 4		± 5	
three-letter words	14	9	4 (+)	1 (+)						
four- ” ”	28	17	9 (5+)	2 (+)						
five- ” ”	36	12	17 (7+)	7 (3+)						
six- ” ”	21	8	6 (2+)	6 (1+)	1 (—)					
seven- ” ”	13	2	4 (—)	3 (—)	2 (—)		2 (+)			
eight- ” ”	4		2 (—)	2 (—)						
ten- ” ”	4			1 (—)	1 (—)		1 (—)		1 (—)	
eleven- ” ”	1			1 (+)						
	121	48	42	23	4		3		1	
		40 %	35 %	19 %	3 %		2 %		1 %	

In the first column of the table the length is noted of the words given that have been misidentified. Words of all lengths, from three-letter words up to eleven-letter words are represented (excepting nine-letter words).

[49] In the following we shall use these terms:
1. a *word given* or a *word presented* = a new word that is presented to the reader on a reading-card;
2. a *misidentification* or a *word assumed* = a word that belongs to previously learnt reading material and which is wrongly suggested by the reader in response to a presented new reading-card.

In the second column we get the number of the misidentifications. In all, there are 121 misidentifications. 36 of these (about 30 %) are five-letter words. In the following six columns we get the length of the words assumed as compared with the words given. The sign = means that the word assumed has the same length as the word given. ± 1 means that the length of the word assumed differs from the length of the word given by one letter—either it is one letter longer or one letter shorter.

Thus line four in the table should be read like this: "There are 21 misidentified six-letter words in the material. Eight of these have been mistaken for other six-letter words. Six have been mistaken for words differing in length by one letter—two of these being seven-letter words (2 +) and four being five-letter words. Six have been mistaken for words differing in length by two letters: one of these is an eight-letter word (1 +); five are four-letter words—and only one has been mistaken for a word differing by three letters, this being a three-letter word (—)."

The table shows:

1. Out of 121 misidentified words 40 % (48) have been mistaken for words of exactly the same length and another 35 % (42) have been mistaken for words that are just one letter shorter of longer. 19 % (23) have been mistaken for words that are two letters shorter or longer and only 6 % (8) for words that are three to five letters shorter or longer.

2. Words shorter than three letters are not misidentified.

3. A word given that is three letters long or more is never mistaken for a word that is shorter than three letters.

4. Apart from this the length of a word assumed does not seem to differ from the length of the corresponding word given by more than about half the number of the letters in the word given.

5. It is evident that the shorter a word given, the more often it is mistaken for a word of exactly the same length:
Among 14 given three-letter words two-thirds have been mistaken for other words of the same length and the rest—with one exception—for words just one letter longer.
More than half of the 28 four-letter words have been mistaken for words of the same length, almost a third for words one letter longer or shorter, and the rest (two words) for those two letters longer.

Distinguishing five- and six-letter words seems also to be quite good, however. More than three-quarters of the five-letter words and two-thirds of the six-letter words have been mistaken for words of the same length or differing by only one letter. Five-letter words have never been mistaken for words differing by more than two letters, and six-letter words have never been mistaken for ones differing by more than three letters (compare above, 4). Seven-letter words might be mistaken for words differing by up to four letters, but still almost half of the misidentified 13 seven-letter words have been mistaken for words not differing by more than one letter.

Nine out of the 121 misidentifications have been made on presented eight- to eleven-letter words. Here the correlation does not seem to be so good; none of the presented words has been mistaken for words of exactly the same length, and the four ten-letter words have been mistaken for words two to five letters shorter.

Thus this investigation of the length of a given new word as compared with the word it is wrongly supposed to be seems to show that the reader is well aware of word-length and that word-length plays an important part in the identification of a word.[50]

Number of letters common to a new word given and the word it is wrongly supposed to be. When the new word *berg* is read as the previously learnt *steg* it is not only the same length of the two words that causes the reader to choose *steg* as a possible reading but also the fact that both words contain the letters *e* and *g*. If a new word is to be mistaken for an already known word, *the two words must have a certain number of letters in common.* The number of these letters seems to depend on the length of the two words.

The following table shows the relations between the number of letters in a new word and the number of letters common to this word and the previously learnt word it is wrongly assumed to be.

[50] Huey in his chapter on "Experimental studies upon visual perception in reading", refers to *Erdmann* and *Dodge*, who are of the opinion that "the length of the word and its characteristic general form as a visual whole seem . . . to be the main means by which it is recognized by the practiced readers" (p. 73). According to Huey, *Zeitler* ascribes less importance to these factors (Huey, p. 85—86). *Messmer,* too, argues against word-length as an important factor. Huey writes: "He finds that word-length plays little part in characterizing words for children, and that it is usually less important for children than are the dominant complexes" (p. 93).

TABLE VI.

Length of new words	Number of letters common to new words and the words they are wrongly assumed to be									
	1	2	3	4	5	6	7	8	9	Average
three-letter words	2	10	2							2 (67 %)
four- ” ”		13	11	4						2.7 (68 %)
five- ” ”	1	7	12	14	2					3.3 (66 %)
six- ” ”		2	4	10	4	1				3.9 (65 %)
seven- ” ”		1	1	6	4	1				4.2 (60 %)
eight- ” ”				1		2	1			5.8 (73 %)
ten- ” ”				1	2		1			5.3 (53 %)
eleven- ” ”									1	

The table shows that the longer a new word, the higher the number of letters common to this word and the previously learnt word it is wrongly supposed to be.

„A new three-letter word is not confused with a previously learnt word if the two words do not have *one* to *three* letters in common: two new three-letter words have *one*, ten have *two*, and two have *three* letters in common with their corresponding misidentifications; the average number of letters in common is *two*, which is 67 % of the new word given. The corresponding numbers are for

four-letter words	two	to	four	letters, average	2.7	(68 %)
five- ” ”	one	to	five	” ”	3.3	(66 %)
six- ” ”	two	to	six	” ”	3.9	(65 %)
seven- ” ”	two	to	six	” ”	4.2	(60 %)
eight- ” ”	four	to	seven	” ”	5.8	(73 %)
ten- ” ”	four	to	seven	” ”	5.3	(53 %)

One eleven-letter word has been mistaken for a word with which it has *nine* letters in common.

These numbers show that when a new word is mistaken for a previously learnt word, *on average 65 % of the letters in the new word are contained in the previously learnt word it is wrongly supposed to be.*

Order and position of letters. When the word *skolan* is mistaken for *skogen* it is not only the fact that both words are six letters long and that both contain the letters *k*, *n*, *o* and *s* which causes the misreading. Another most important reason is that the letters common to the words appear in exactly the same order in both, namely *s*, *k*, *o* and *n*.

Investigating our material we find that in only 12 out of the 121 cases of misidentification the order between the common letters is not the same in the new word given as in the word it is assumed to be, e.g. when *berg* is read as *brev* (er:re), or *kliver* is assumed to be *silver* (liv:ily). Thus in 91 % of the 121 cases the order between the letters is the same in both words. We therefore find that the reader has not only a good appreciation of the length of words (see p. 41 ff.) and an ability to recognize letters (see p. 43 f.); he also has a keen appreciation of the order of letters in words.[51]

The "density" of the letters common to a new word given and the word it is wrongly supposed to be may vary. Either the common letters are concentrated in the words or they are spread out. In the three pairs *skägg — skärt, mil — bil, runda — kunde* the common letters are concentrated; in the first example they are concentrated to the beginning of, in the second to the end of, and in the third within both words. In the pairs *älg — äng, bonden — bordet* the common letters are spread out.

There seems to be a rather high congruence as to density between the words given and their misidentifications, as is evident from the following table.

TABLE VII.

	Number of word pairs	Average length of word in letters		Longest word		
		Given	Assumed	Given	Assumed	Neither
A. Letters concentrated in both words	48	4.5	4.5	11	16	21
B. Letters spread out in both words	45	5.8	5.6	15	7	23
C. Letters concentrated in word given, spread out in word assumed	9	4.6	5.1	2	5	2
D. Letters spread out in word given, concentrated in word assumed	19	6.3	4.6	17	—	2

[51] This goes contrary to Zeitler, who considers that a word is seen in certain dominant parts, but that the individual letters are not seen in any very fixed spatial arrangement. "The mere optical word-form is continually inclined to fall apart into its elements, is held together only by the framework formed by the dominating letters. In this word-form the small and unimportant letters can be changed about quite irregularly," and "each dominating letter has a certain elbow-room in a space within which it can be changed about with its neighbours" (Zeitler as quoted by Huey, p. 87).

In 48 cases the common letters are concentrated in both the word given and the word assumed, in 45 cases they are spread out in both. That means that we find *congruence as to density in 77 % of the 121 misidentifications.*

In nine cases the common letters are concentrated in the word given and spread out in the word assumed, in 19 cases the opposite is the case.

Table VII also shows us the relation between the density of the common letters and *the length of the words.* When the common letters are concentrated, the average length of the word is 4.5 to 4.6 letters (see the table, Average length of word in letters). When the letters are spread out, however, the average length of the word varies between 5.1 and 6.3 letters (average: 5.7 letters).

In 48 cases the common letters are concentrated in both the word given and the word assumed: in almost half of these (21 cases) the word given and the word assumed are of exactly same length; in 11 cases the word given is longer, and in 16 cases the word assumed is longer (see table VII, Longest word). The average length of the two groups of words is exactly the same.

Also in half of those 45 cases where the common letters are spread out in both words, the word given and the word assumed are of exactly the same length. In 15 cases the word given is the longer, in seven cases the word assumed. The average length of the word given is 5.8 letters, that of the word assumed 5.6 letters; the difference might be considered as insignificant.

There are only nine cases where the common letters are concentrated in the word given and spread out in the word assumed. In five—that is more than half—of these cases the word assumed—that is the "spread" one—is longer. The difference between average lengths is very slight, however, only 0.5 letters.

In those 19 cases where the letters are spread out in the word given and concentrated in the word assumed, the word given—that is the "spread" one—is almost invariably the longer: in 17 out of 19 cases. The difference between the average lengths is considerable: the given, "spread" word is on average 1.7 letters longer than the assumed, "concentrated" word.

Now, returning to *skolan,* which was assumed to be the previously learnt *skogen,* the common letters are here spread out in the two words; moreover the position of the common letters is exactly the same in *skolan* as in *skogen*: $\dfrac{skolan}{skogen}$. It seems plausible that this fact may be of importance for the misidentification. Having common letters in the same positions the two words make a similar visual impression on the reader if he takes them in as whole entities, without detailed analysis. Thus it must be of great interest to examine the positions of the common letters in the words given as compared with the words assumed. To be able to do this, however, we must find a way of describing these positions.

A rather inexact way of describing positions is to use such terms as "beginning", "end" and "within". To begin with, however, we will use that mode of description.

We exclude two groups from the investigation:

1. Those words which are "incongruent as to density", i.e. where the common letters are concentrated in the word given and spread out in the word assumed or vice versa. Ex. *ske*na — *ske*den, klu*nkar* — b*rukar*. Here the position of common letters must needs be different in the word given and the word assumed. 23 % of the 121 misidentifications belong to this group.

2. Such words as are congruent as to density but where the word given is contained in the word assumed or vice versa: ex. *dör — dör*r, *låter — åter*. 6 % of the 11 misidentifications are of this kind.

When these two groups have been excluded, 71 % of the 121 misidentifications are left. These are all "congruent as to density". The position of common letters in these words is as follows:

Same position in both words	66	(54 %)
Concentrated	34	(28 %)
Beginning	12	(10 %)
End	19	(16 %)
Within	3	(2 %)
Spread out	32	(26 %)
Beginning — End	19	(16 %)
Beginning — Within	3	(2 %)
Within — End	9	(7 %)
Within — Within	1	(1 %)
Different positions in the two words	20	(17 %)
Concentrated		
(beginning of word given—end of word assumed, etc.)	7	(6 %)
Spread out		
(beginning and end of word given—within and end of word		
assumed, etc.)	13	(11 %)

From this table we see that in 66 out of the 121 misidentifications, that is 54 %, the common letters appear in the same parts of both the word given and the word assumed. Furthermore we see that the common letters very often appear at the beginning and/or at the end of both words. In 50 out of the 66 "congruent" pairs the common letters appear only in these positions.

That the beginning and end of the words are of great importance to the reader also becomes evident if we examine the positions of common letters in all 121 cases of misidentification. 81 words given have common letters at the end, 69 at the beginning and 50 within. 96 words assumed have common letters at the end, 71 at the beginning and only 36 within.[52]

To get a measure of the degree of similarity between a word given and the word it is assumed to be, the rough way of describing position used above is insufficient. By this method *mätte* read as *tvätt* is classed in the "incongruent" group because of the final *e* in *mätte*: the common letters are "within" the word given and at the end of the word assumed.

When *undrar* is mistaken for *hundra*, the common letters are at the "beginning" of the word given and at the "end" of the word assumed, but the difference between the two words really does not seem as great as the terms "beginning" and "end" indicate.

We should therefore try to find a new and more exact method of describing positions. This method should take into account the length of the two words, the number of common letters and the order of these letters, thus making it possible to find a measure indicating the degree of similarity between a word given and its misidentification and including as many factors as possible.

To find such a method we had better first study some misidentifications.

If the new word *sönder* is wrongly supposed to be the previously learnt *gömmer*, we say that the misidentification is due to the fact that both words have the same length, that both words contain *ö* and *er*, and that these common letters have the same position in both words.

We might also suppose that when the reader was first presented with the word *gömmer*, for some reason he focused his attention on *ö* and *er*, that to him those letters were the dominating parts of the words,[53] and that after having "learnt" the word the reader had an overall

---

[52] Needless to say, those having common letters at the beginning might also have such at the end and within—that is why the sum of the words is not 121.

[53] Compare above p. 24 f. "*mage* liknar *öga*" "*precis* liknar *pappa*", and my analysis of these two comments.

impression of the length and the "look" of the word, plus a clear imaginary picture of the letters *ö* and *er* within and at the end of the word.

The reader's "memory image" of *gömmer* might be represented like this: *(g)ö(mm)er*, the parentheses indicating that *g* and *mm* stand out less clearly.[54] Now, being presented with the word *sönder*, the reader recognizes the letters *ö* and *er*, the dominating parts of the word *gömmer*. Moreover, in *sönder ö* and *er* appear in the same "setting" as in *gömmer*: *gömmer* and *sönder* are both six letters long, *ö* being the second letter and *e* and *r* the two last letters in both words. So *sönder* is wrongly supposed to be *gömmer*. The misidentification might be illustrated in the following way:

	1 2 34 56
New word given	*(s)ö(nd) er*
Old remembered word	*(g)ö(mm)er*

Here each word has six positions: three corresponding positions, 2, 5 and 6, contain the same letters, and three corresponding positions, 1, 3 and 4, contain different letters. We might say that the pair *sönder — gömmer* taken as a whole fills up six positions, three of which are identical and three of which are contrasting.

Now, let us consider the word *tunnel*, which has been read *tung*.

	123 456
New word given	*tun (ne l)*
Old remembered word	*tun (g--)*

The dominating part causing the misidentification is *tun*. This fills up the first three positions in both words, which positions are thus identical. But the rest of the word given contrasts with the rest of the word assumed in that *n* is opposed by *g*, *e* by a blank and *l* by a blank. Thus

---

[54] *Goldscheider* and *Müller* have found that "an optical memory image" of a word is readily called forth by an incomplete series of its letters. They make a distinction between "determining letters" (letters which seem to be especially used in determining the recognition of any given word) and "indifferent letters" (Huey, p. 79). *Zeitler* in his experiments "found that in his brief exposure certain letters or letter-groups of a word, and indeed certain words of exposed sentences, drew the attention to themselves and were apperceived. The apperception of these dominating parts or complexes is, he believes, the basis for the recognition of the word or sentence. These apperceived parts are at once supplemented by, filled out with, an inner mental contribution, associates that belong with the parts apperceived. The result is the blending of the outwardly given apperceptions with the inwardly arising associates into a total 'assimilation', which constitutes the recognition of the word or sentence. 'The word-form is indeed apparently assimilated as a whole, *secondarily;* but *primarlily* it is apperceived only in its dominating constituent parts.' " (Huey, p. 82—83.)

we might say that the pair *tunnel — tung* taken as a whole fills up six positions, three of which are identical and three of which are contrasting. This is exactly like the pair *sönder — gömmer* above, the only difference being that in *tunnel — tung* two of the contrasting elements are 0.

Now, in both examples above the letters common to the word given and the word assumed have the same "density". In *sönder — gömmer* they are spread out, in *tunnel — tung* they are *concentrated*. In 23 % of the misidentifications, however, word given and word assumed are "incongruent" as to density.

We have already seen (p. 45 table VII above) that a "spread" word is more often mistaken for a "concentrated" one than vice versa. When the new *stygga* is mistaken for the earlier learnt *nya*, the dominating parts are *y* and *a*. We might suppose that the reader remembers *nya* essentially as *y* and *a* with something before *y*: *(n)ya*. When he meets *stygga*, he recognizes *y* and *a*. Here again there is something before *y*: *(st)y*, But in *stygga* there are also two letters between *y* and *a*, and to read *stygga* as *nya* the reader must "overlook" these two letters:

$$12 \ 3 \ 45 \ 6$$
$$(st)y(gg)a$$
$$(-n)y(--)a.$$

Using the same positional table as in the earlier examples we might say that taken as a whole the two words have six positions, two of which (numbers 3 and 6) are identical and four contrasting.[55]

When *torka* is read as *tror* a "concentrated" word is mistaken for a "spread" one. The dominating parts are here *t* and *or*. The reader remembers *tror* essentially as *t* and *or* with something in between: *t(r)or* When he is confronted with *torka*, he recognizes *t* and *or*. But here there is nothing between *t* and *or*. To confuse *torka* with *tror* the reader must somehow "imagine" something between these two parts of the word presented:

$$1 \ 2 \ 34 \ 56$$
$$t(-)or(ka)$$
$$t(r)or(--).$$

It seems to me that it is a more difficult process to "imagine" than to "overlook" (as was the case with the type represented by *stygga — nya*

---

[55] As to the first two positions—in *stygga* occupied by *s* and *t*, in *nya* by *n* and a blank— it is not possible to say which of the two letters *s* and *t* contrasts with *n* and which with the blank. Theoretically there are two possibilities: (st)y (gg)a   (st)y (gg)a
(-n)y (--)a   or   (n-)y (--)a.
The same is true of *tunnel — tung* above.

above). This might be the reason why a "spread" word is more often mistaken for a "dense" one than a "dense" word for a "spread" one. Another important fact is that in 10 out of 19 cases under D above (p. 45 table VII) where a "spread" word is mistaken for a "concentrated" one, the old remembered "concentrated" word is totally included in the new "spread" one, which must reinforce the tendency to "over-looking": ex. *halv* is read as *hav*, *mörkret* as *mörkt*, *ärter* as *äter* etc.

Returning to *torka — tror* above and using the same positional table as earlier, we might say that taken as a whole the two words have six positions, three of which (numbers 1, 3 and 4) are identical and three contrasting.

Let us sum up what has been said above about the new words and the previously learnt words they are wrongly supposed to be, the "misidentifications". A word given and the word it is assumed to be have certain letters in common. These letters seem to be the dominating parts on which the misidentification partly depends. Other important factors are the length of the two words (see p. 41 ff.) and the order of the common letters (see p. 44 ff.). While aware of the drawbacks, we made a rough description of the positions of the common letters using the terms "beginning", "end" and "within". Even this first investigation showed that the position of common letters is strikingly similar in words given and the words these are mistaken for.

We have tried to find a new way to measure the degree of similarity between a word given and the word it is assumed to be, a way which would take into account all these important facts: length of word, letters in common, order of common letters and position of common letters. In trying to find such a method we have started with the common letters as the dominating parts of the misidentifications, making a positional schedule where the word assumed is written below the word given in such a way that every letter which the word assumed has in common with the word given is written below the corresponding letter of the word given.

```
1 2  34 56      123 456       12 3 45 6     1 2 34 56
(s)ö (n d)er    tun(ne l)     (st)y(gg)a    t(-)or(ka)
(g)ö(mm)er      tun(g--)      (-n)y(--)a    t(r)or(--)
```

The number of positions with common letters—called identical positions—represents the similarity between the words; the number of positions with contrasting letters (or positions where a letter in one word is represented by a blank in the other)—called contrasting position—represents the difference between the words.

To get a measure of the degree of similarity between the two words we might divide the number of identical positions by the total number of positions:[56] $\dfrac{Pi}{Pt}$.

This method of measuring takes into account the length of the word given and of the word assumed.

Ex. 1 234
$(t)ack$ $\dfrac{Pi}{Pt} = \dfrac{3}{4} = 0.75$
$(b)ack$

1 234 56
$(t)ack(ar)$ $\dfrac{Pi}{Pt} = \dfrac{3}{6} = 0.50$
$(b)ack(en)$

In both pairs above, the word given and the word assumed have three letters in common: these letters appear in the same order in both words and they are "congruently" placed in each pair, concentrated at the end of the first pair, concentrated within the second pair. That $\dfrac{Pi}{Pt}$ is higher for the first pair than for the second is due only to the fact that the words of the second pair are longer than those of the first one, which means that the percentage of common letters is lower in the second pair.

The method considers the common letters only as far as they appear in the same order in the word given and the word assumed.

Ex. $\dfrac{ki(tt)lar}{ki(--)lar}$ $\dfrac{Pi}{Pt} = \dfrac{5}{7} = 0.71$ $\dfrac{k(-)i(ttl)ar}{k(l)i(---)ar}$ $\dfrac{Pi}{Pt} = \dfrac{4}{8} = 0.50$

The two pairs above have both five letters in common, and in both pairs the word given is seven letters long and the word assumed five letters long; but the first pair has $\dfrac{Pi}{Pt} = 0.71$, the second pair only $\dfrac{Pi}{Pt} = 0.50$ owing to the reversed order $il - li$ there, which gives two additional contrasting positions in the schedule.

Finally the method also considers the density of the common letters. The pair $\dfrac{(h)a(s)p}{(r)a(m)p}$ where the common letters are congruently spread in both words, gets a $\dfrac{Pi}{Pt} = \dfrac{2}{4} = 0.50$; the pair $\dfrac{(h)a(s)p(-)}{(l)a(-)p(a)}$ gets a $\dfrac{Pi}{Pt} = \dfrac{2}{5} = 0.40$ because here the common letters are spread out in the word

[56] Pi = positions identical, Pt = positions totally.

given and concentrated in the word assumed.

The pair $\dfrac{ap(or)}{ap(an)}$ has $\dfrac{Pi}{Pt} = \dfrac{2}{4} = 0.50$, but $\dfrac{(-)ap\,(or)}{(l)\,ap\,(p\text{-})}$ has $\dfrac{Pi}{Pt} = \dfrac{2}{5} =$

$= 0.40$.

In the first case the common letters are concentrated at the beginning of both words, in the second case the common letters are at the beginning of the word given and within the word assumed.

The method also gives us an opportunity of making finer distinctions as regards positions than do the terms "beginning", "end" and "within".

The two pairs $\dfrac{(br)\ddot{a}tt(e)}{(sl)\,\ddot{a}tt(\text{-})} \quad \dfrac{(\text{-}r)\ddot{a}tt(er)}{(sl)\,\ddot{a}tt(\text{--})}$ would with these terms both be

classified as: word given six letters long, word assumed five letters long, three concentrated common letters within the word given and at the end of the word assumed. The common-sense evaluation that the words in the first pair are more similar than those in the second one is confirmed, however, by the $\dfrac{Pi}{Pt}$, which is 0.50 for the first pair and 0.43 for the second.

Now $\dfrac{Pi}{Pt}$ for a given word and the word it is wrongly supposed to be can never be as high as 1. $\dfrac{Pi}{Pt} = 1$ implies that all positions are identical, i.e. the word given = the word assumed, which means that we have a correct reading. What then is the maximum of $\dfrac{Pi}{Pt}$? The answer is that the maximum varies with the length of the word given. We always get the highest degree of similarity if the word given is included in the word assumed and the word assumed is only one letter longer than the word given. The maximal $\dfrac{Pi}{Pt}$ is thus for a given three-letter word $\dfrac{3}{4} =$

0.75, for a four-letter word $\dfrac{4}{5} = 0.80$, for a five-letter word $\dfrac{5}{6} = 0.83$ etc.

Thus $\dfrac{Pi}{Pt}$ for *lat — lata* is lower (0.75) than for *prat — prata* (0.80) not because there is greater similarity between the words in the second pair than between those in the first one, but because the word presented in the second pair is longer than that in the first one.

So if we are to compare the degree of similarity within different pairs of words given and words assumed on the basis of $\frac{Pi}{Pt}$ we are obliged to reduce the difference in $\frac{Pi}{Pt}$ due only to the varying length of the word assumed. This is done by dividing the $\frac{Pi}{Pt}$ for every pair by the possible maximum for the word given in that pair. If we call this new measure of similarity between word given and word assumed S, we get $S = \frac{Pi}{Pt} : Max\frac{Pi}{Pt}$. Ex. word given $= lat$, word assumed $= lata$. $\frac{Pi}{Pt} = \frac{3}{4} = 0.75$. Max$\frac{Pi}{Pt}$ for given three-letter word ($lata$) $= \frac{3}{4} = 0.75$. $S = \frac{0.75}{0.75} = 1$. Word given $prat$, word assumed $prata$. $\frac{Pi}{Pt} = \frac{4}{5} = 0.80$. Max $\frac{Pi}{Pt}$ for given four-letter word (prat) $= \frac{4}{5} = 0.80$. $S = \frac{0.80}{0.80} = 1$.

In this way it is established that the degree of similarity between lat and $lata$ is as high as that between $prat$ and $prata$.

The table below shows us how the degree of similarity between word given and word assumed in our material varies with the length of the word given.

TABLE VIII.

Length in letters of word given	Number of words in the material	Medium S
3	14	0.69
4	28	0.74
5	36	0.69
6	21	0.69
7	13	0.60
8	4	0.77
10	4	0.58
11	1	0.75

On the basis of the medium S values in the table above we may also calculate an average medium S for all the words presented and their misidentifications. This average medium S is 0.69.

From the table we see that S varies from 0.58 to 0.77. *A priori* one would suppose that the greatest degree of similarity would be found when the word presented is a short one, the lowest degree when the word presented is long. In this table, however, both the highest S values and the lowest are to be found when the word given is a long one. The ten-letter words have the lowest S (0.58), the eight-letter words and the eleven-letter words the highest (0.77 and 0.75). It is to be observed, however, that these groups appear very rarely: four given eight-letter words, four given ten-letter words and only one given eleven-letter word. The better represented groups have their S nearer the medium figure 0.69. In order to compare S for words given of different lengths we had better arrange the words so as to get groups of about the same size.

TABLE IX.

Length in letters of word given	Number of words in the material	Medium S
3 and 4	42	0.71
5	36	0.69
6 to 11	43	0.68

From this rearranged table we see that S—which is the degree of similarity between the word given and the word it is assumed to be—is surprisingly constant. There is some tendency, however, towards a lesser degree of similarity when the word given becomes longer.

Similar letters. When *bada* is mistaken for *båda* or *haka* for *kaka* $\frac{Pi}{Pt}$ for both pairs is $\frac{3}{4} = 0.75$ and S is 0.94. Also if *varm* is mistaken for *larm* we get $\frac{Pi}{Pt} = 0.75$ and S = 0.94. Nevertheless, it is obvious that there is greater resemblance between *haka* and *kaka*, and between *bada* and *båda*, than between *varm* and *larm*. The reason is evident: the contrasting graphemes *a* and *å*, *h* and *k* are more similar than the contrasting graphemes *v* and *l*.

Now, is there any way of deciding the degree of similarity between different letters?

In his paper "*Förhållandet mellan skrift och tal*" Sture Allén, after having made a distinction between syngraphemes and autographemes (cf. p. 90), groups the autographemes according to their distinctive features (Allén, p. 79, figure 3) in the following way:

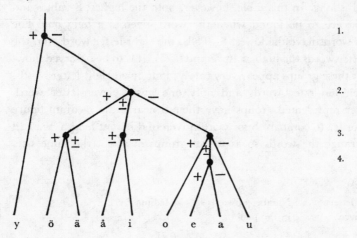

The plus and minus signs should be interpreted as follows

		+	±	—
1.	steeple	with		without
2.	diacritical signs	two	one	none
3.	loop	big	small	none
4.	vertical position of loop	above		below

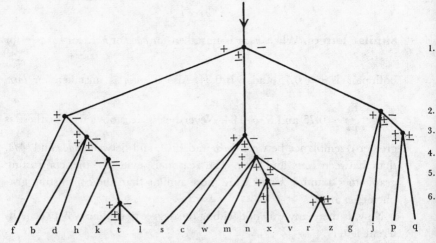

Allén then says it is also possible to group the syngraphemes according to their distinctive features. He has kindly offered me a copy of his as yet (December 1970) unpublished analysis of the syngraphemes. Allén's "tree" showing the distictive features of the syngraphemes of modern Swedish is given at the bottom of page 64. The plus and minus signs should be interpreted as follows:

	+	+	+	—	—
	+	—		—	
1. Direction of steeple		upwards	none	down-wards	
2. Form of steeple		loop	bent	straight	
3. Direction of convexity	right	right and left	left	none	
4. Number of low steeples	four	three	two	one	null
5. Points of contact of low steeples		above	central	below	
6. Direction of by-strokes		right	right and left	none	

If we look at Sture Allén's two graphs we find groups of graphemes that are "similar" because the members of the group have some of their distinctive features in common. Among the autographemes only *ö*, *ä*, *å* and *i* have diacritical signs, but of these four *ö*, *ä* and *å* have another distinctive feature in common: they have all a loop. Among the syngraphemes we have three big groups: those with a steeple going up, those with a steeple going down, and those without steeple.

Applied to the reading process and to the reader's ability to distinguish between graphemes, this analysis into distinctive features raises the following problem: what distinctive features are p s y c h o l o g i c a l l y r e l e v a n t to the reader? To find this out I have gone through all the misidentifications observing s i n g l e c o n t r a s t i n g g r a p h e m e s i n c o r r e s p o n d i n g p o s i t i o n s .

When the new words and the words they are mistakenly supposed by the reader to be differ by single contrasting graphemes in the same positions, the misidentifications are probably more easily made if these single contrasting graphemes are s i m i l a r . It may be supposed that *bada* is more easily confused with *båda* than *bada* with *bida*. Then, by exam-

TABLE X.

Given \ Supposea →	Autographemes									Syngraphemes: steeple upwards							no steeple									steeple downwards			
	y	ö	ä	å	i	o	e	a	u	f	b	d	h	k	t	l	s	c	w	m	n	x	v	r	z	g	j	p	q
Autographemes y																													
ö																													
ä																													
å					1																					1			
i																													
o																													
e								1																					
a							1		1																				
u							1		1																				
Syngraphemes steeple upwards f										2	2		1	1		1										1			
b											1	1	1		1	1										1			
d												1	1		1	2													
h												1	5		1	1													
k													1	1	1	3							2			1			
t															1								1						
l															1	1								1		1			
no steeple s																									1				
c																													
w																													
m																													
n																													
x																													
v																							1						
r																													
z																	1									1			
steeple downwards g										1			1			1													
j																													
p																													
q																													

ining the single contrasting graphemes you may get a measure of what graphemes are most easily mixed up, i.e. the similarity between graphemes as observed by the reader.

Only single contrasting graphemes in corresponding positions have been noted, which means that $\dfrac{haka}{kaka} \dfrac{varm}{larm}$ etc. have been taken into account, whereas the type $\dfrac{slags}{d\ ags}$ has not been noted. The reason is that when *slags* is supposed to be *dags*, you might say either that *s* contrasts with *d* and *l* with null or that *s* contrasts with null and *l* with *d*. For the same reason $\dfrac{bada}{b\aa da}$, $\dfrac{liv}{lov}$ have been taken into account, but not $\dfrac{banta}{bad\ a}$. Also $\dfrac{sil}{sin}$ has been noted but not $\dfrac{Tom}{Tora}$. The result of this investigation is shown in table X on page 58.

Only 42 cases of single contrasting positions have been found. No conclusions have been drawn from such single instances as when a *u* was incidentally mistaken for an *a*. Apart from these the table shows some very clear tendencies:

1. Autographemes contrast with autographemes, syngraphemes with syngraphemes. The only exception is when an *a* incidentally contrasts with a *g* in *lånat — långt*.
2. As regards the syngraphemes, the steeple seems to be a most important distinctive feature. In the words given we have 36 syngraphemes in single contrasting positions, 31 of which have a steeple. Out of these, 25 contrast with syngraphemes containing a steeple in the supposed word. If we consider each syngrapheme we get the following result:

d All four contrast with syngraphemes that have steeples: in three cases the steeple goes upwards, in one it goes downwards (*g*).

h All five contrast with syngraphemes that have steeples going upwards.

k Both contrast with syngraphemes that have steeples going upwards.

l Seven out of ten contrast with syngraphemes that have steeples going upwards.

t Five out of six contrast with syngraphemes that have steeples; in four cases the steeple goes upwards, in one case it goes downwards.

g Two out of four contrast with syngraphemes that have steeples going upwards.

3. The syngraphemes without steeples show no clear tendencies.

4. For the **autographemes** the material is very scanty. It seems, however, as if *a* tends to be confused with *å* and *ä*. From this we may draw the conclusion that autographemes which only differ by diacritical signs are more easily confused than others.[57]

Following the indications of this preliminary investigation, we thus decide that the following graphemes should be regarded as similar:

1. *a/å/ä*;

2. *o/ö* (although no examples have been found in the scanty material of single letters in contrasting position, I have supposed this to be true in analogy with *a/ä*);

3. all syngraphemes with steeples going upwards, and *g*.

Now, once more going through the 121 words given and their misidentifications, we decide that with each pair where a grapheme in the word given corresponds to a "similar" grapheme in the word assumed, and where these graphemes are situated at the same side of identical graphemes in both words, the word pair should get one extra point as to similarity.

Ex. Word	pairs	Similar letters	
lös	— hus	l	— h
drog	— tog	d	— t
halv	— själv	a	— ä
elva	— enda	l	— d

[57] The tendencies noted here are confirmed by *Zeitler*'s experiments. He has found that the letters projecting above and below the line are recognized especially (Huey, p. 83). *Messmer* has found "that the long letters which project above the line are usually the dominating ones". Moreover: "The attention concerns itself most with the upper half of the word, and the letters projecting below are not so important" (Huey, p. 91). Huey himself has experimentally found that "The upper half of a word or letter is obviously more important for perception than is the lower half" (p. 98). The graphemes with steeples going upwards are then to be considered as dominating parts of their words, and they are dominating on account of their common distinctive feature—the steeple going upwards. According to this a presented new word containing a grapheme with a steeple going upwards could quite easily be confused with an already learnt word which contains another grapheme with steeple going upwards, if the graphemes are situated in similar positions in both words.—Problems of graphical similarity are also discussed by *Karl-Hampus Dahlstedt* in "*Homonymi i nusvenskan*" (*Nysvenska Studier* 1965).

förstörd — förstod	ö — o
bestämt — bästa	ä — a
leta — hela	l, t — h, l
gått — hatt	g, å — h, a

TABLE XI.

Length of word given	Total number of word pairs	Number of word pairs with similar letters	Number of word pairs with *one* similar letter	Number of word pairs with *two* similar letters
3 and 4-letter words	42	23 (55 %)	21 (50 %)	2 (5 %)
5-letter words	36	14 (39 %)	11 (30 %)	3 (9 %)
6 to 11-letter words	43	21 (49 %)	17 (40 %)	4 (9 %)
	121	58 (47 %)	49 (40 %)	9 (7 %)

The 121 word pairs have been gone through and the number of word pairs containing similar letters has been calculated. The result can be seen in table XI.

The table shows that 58—that is 47 %—of the 121 word pairs, where a new word presented is mistaken for a previously learnt word, contain similar letters. In 49 word pairs (40 %) there is only one similar letter, e.g. *lös — hus;* in the nine other word pairs (7 %) there are two similar letters, e.g. *leta — hela.*

The word pairs have been grouped according to the length of the given word in the same way as was done in table IX on page 55, when the degree of similarity was decided on the basis of common letters, position of common letters and word-length.

It seems as if there were a certain tendency towards a greater frequency of similar letters in word pairs where the word given is short (three to four letters). This would to some extent contradict what is said above, p. 55: that the degree of similarity between a word given and the word it is mistaken for seems to be rather constant whatever the length of the word given. Instead it gives support to the weak tendency noted towards a lesser degree of similarity when the word given becomes longer—this tendency is also supported by the fact that there are only one or two similar letters (in about the same proportions) in the word pairs where the given word is three, four or five letters long, as well as in the word pairs where the given word is six to eleven letters long: one similar letter out of three gives a greater degree of similarity than one out of eleven.

Chapter Seven
Third period (April 1ˢᵗ 1966—Oct. 31ˢᵗ 1966): Analytical readings of morphemes

The growing reading skill—that is the gradual development towards an insight into the grapho-phonematic correspondences, and a capacity for using this insight actively when reading new words—is reflected in the analytical readings. In the description (pp. 29–32 above) of the first analytical readings in March, we find that both independent and dependent morphemes are involved in the processes. In the case of *jadå* the independent morpheme *då* is added to the base *ja*; in *pengarna* the dependent morpheme *-na* is added to *pengar*. Analytical readings with only independent morphemes might be considered as comparatively easy, because these morphemes may occur as separate graphic entities. The handling of dependent morphemes is, however, a bit more complicated, as these only occur tied to other morphemes. The reader must thus be able to abstract the dependent morphemes from previously learnt words in order to cope with them in analytical readings of new words presented.[58]

A. Analytical readings with simple dependent morphemes

Quite naturally there are rather few analytical readings where only independent morphemes are implied: the independent morphemes ("words") and their combinations are innumerable but of relatively low frequency. The dependent morphemes, however, are few, enumerable and very frequent, inevitably being used to mark certain grammatical relations in sentences. Thus a great many of the analytical readings imply adjunction, deletion or substitution of d e p e n d e n t m o r p h e m e s. In this chapter we are going to treat the analytical readings of dependent morphemes, as these readings are most revealing about the problem of how reading ability is gradually acquired.

The dependent morphemes are only gradually mastered. In the table below we have a survey of the use of s i m p l e d e p e n d e n t morphemes

---

[58] With those dependent morphemes which have independent homographs, such as *-en* with the homograph *en*, this difficulty is absent; compare p. 66 below.

in analytical readings during the different months. The first appearance of a morpheme is marked with an italicized *x*.

We have already shown (p. 30) that the reason why the morpheme *-na* is mastered in March—and the girl can read *pengarna* by adding the previously learnt *pengar* and *-na*—is that patterns in her earlier reading material enable her to identify *-na* both graphically and semantically: *kattungar* and *kattungarna*. Moreover there are other words in her reading vocabulary ending in *-na*: *fjärilarna, fåglarna, tassarna, blommorna, grodorna,* and *insekterna*.

As a rule the patterns in the earlier material which enable the reader to identify a new word presented are both morphological and semantical: on the 4th of April the new *våta* is read correctly because it is the sum of the basic independent morpheme *våt*—here an adjective—which is already known, and the dependent morpheme *-a* forming the plural and definite singular of adjectives. This *-a* can be drawn from the previously learnt, morphologically and semantically parallel, adjective forms *snäll — snälla, ihålig — ihåliga* etc.

TABLE XII.

	March	April	May	June	July	Sept.	Oct.
-a	x	x	x	x	x	x	x
-an		x			x	x	x
-ande				x		x	
-ar	x	x	x	x	x	x	x
-are			x	x		x	x
-d				x		x	
-de	x	x	x	x	x	x	x
-e			x	x	x	x	x
-el							x
-en	x	x	x	x	x	x	x
-er		x	x	x	x	x	x
-et			x	x	x	x	x
-ig			x				
-ing			x				
-is					x		
-it					x		
-n				x	x	x	x
-na	x	x	x	x	x	x	x
-or		x	x	x	x	x	x
-r		x	x	x	x	x	x
-s	x		x	x	x	x	x
-t		x	x	x	x	x	x
-te				x		x	x

The patterns may not necessarily be semantical, however. When *höga* is read correctly in June by deleting the *-n* from the previously learnt *högan*, where *-n* is part of a dependent morpheme forming an obsolete adjective form, the patterns are drawn from noun pairs like *flicka — flickan, mamma — mamman* etc. in which the morpheme *-n* marks the definite singular form of the noun.

In a few cases a correct analytical reading is due to homography, as when the infinitive *sköta* (nurse) is read correctly as a sum of a previously learnt homographic strong preterite, *sköt* (shot), and the morpheme *-a*, drawn from word pairs like *läs — läsa, gör — göra* etc.

The patterns may also inspire correct readings on account of homography where no real morphemes are implied, as when in June *fönsterruta* (*fönster* = window, *ruta* = pane) is read as the sum of *fönster* + *ut* + *a*,[59] where *-a* is mastered because of earlier patterns and readings in which *-a* is a dependent morpheme. There are four more readings of this kind in the material. They have all been treated as analytical readings containing a dependent morpheme.

Now, if we consider all the 23 dependent morphemes listed in the table above being mastered successively through the months—what are their patterns and when do these patterns appear?

18 out of 23 dependent morphemes have clear patterns. As a rule these patterns appear in the reading material one to three months before the first corresponding analytical readings are made—this is true of 16 out of the 18 morphemes with clear patterns: *-a, -an, -ar, -are, -e, -el, -en, -er, -et, -it, -n, -na, -or, -s, -t,* and *-te.*

E. g. *före* is read correctly in May by adjunction of the previously learnt *för* and *-e*; this *-e* is probably extracted from *ut* and *ute*, appearing for the first time in the reading material presented in March. The word *höga* is read in June by deleting the *n* in the previously learnt *högan*; graphical patterns are found already in March, when the reading material contains words like *flicka — flickan, mamma — mamman, nästa — nästan.*

The morpheme *-r*, however, appears for the first time in an analytical reading in April but has patterns as much as four months earlier. On the first of April *stanna* is read correctly by deletion of *-r* from the previously learnt *stannar.* The girl herself has confirmed the process by reading "*stannar . . . stanna*" and by adding "*Jag har haft stannar*" (I have had *stannar*). Patterns for the reading are found in *ha — har, se — ser,*

---

[59] The homography is not complete, the double *r* being treated as a single one.

titta — tittar, fråga — frågar, få — får, ge — ger, gå — går etc. The pattern *ha — har* appears as early as December.

In one case the patterns for an analytical reading of a dependent morpheme are not older than a couple of weeks (they appear earlier in the same month). This is true of the morpheme *-de*. In March (on the 25ᵗʰ) *hittade* is read *hittde* on the base of *hittat* and *fråga — frågade*; probably the homographic independent morpheme *de* (third personal plural pronoun), which is very frequent in the reading material, also helps the girl to identify the graphical sequence *-de* in *hittade*. Graphical patterns for identifying and deleting *-t* in *hittat* are found in February: *fin — fint, ihålig — ihåligt — ihåliga, snäll — snällt — snälla*. In spite of this, the substitution is incorrect.

Five simple dependent morphemes appear in analytical readings for which no patterns may be found. This is the case with *-ig* and *-ing* used only in May, *-ande* and *-d* which first appear in June, and *-is* used only in July. We shall examine these five instances in detail.

-ig: *väldigt* (May 17ᵗʰ) is read correctly as an adjunction *väl+d+ig+t*. Already in January a lot of adjectives in the plural form *-iga* are presented: *duniga, hungriga, lurviga* etc. The morpheme *-a* is mastered as early as March, and *-ig* might thus be read by deleting *-a* from *-iga*.

-ing: *trehjuling* (May 16ᵗʰ) is read as an adjunction *tre+jul+ing*.[60] The pronoun *ingen*, frequent early, and the morpheme *-en*, which is mastered already in March, make it possible to regard *-ing* as the result of a deletion *ing(en)*.

-ande: *klappade* (June 9ᵗʰ) is read as *klappande*. Earlier *klappar* has been learnt. Here *-ar*, which is mastered since March, had been substituted by *-ande* instead of the correct *-ade*. Probably *-ade* has been mistaken for *-an* (mastered in April) and *-de* (mastered in March). The incorrect reading *-ande* might thus be explained as the result of an adjunction.

-d: *gömd* (June 7ᵗʰ) is read correctly on the base of *gömmer* by the substitution *gömm-er/-d*; the *d* might be seen as the result of a deletion of *e—* mastered in May—from *de*.

-is: *björkris* (July 21ˢᵗ) is read as *börjis*, i.e. *-ade* in the already well-known *började* is substituted by *-is*—a morpheme which was at that time uncommonly frequent in the girl's spoken language for making new words of

---

[60] The *h* is overlooked, but the result is correct because *hj* and *j* are both pronounced [j] in Swedish.

a slangy character. Graphically -*is* might be seen as an adjunction of *i*— well known as an independent morpheme (preposition) which is in context almost always pronounced s h o r t—and -*s* which is mastered as a morpheme already in March.

To sum up: when dependent morphemes first occur in analytical readings they have e i t h e r well established patterns in the earlier reading material (18 out of 23) or they might themselves be explained as the product of analytical readings on the base of earlier reading material: -*ig*(*a*), *ing*(*en*), -*an*+*de*, -*d*(*e*) and -*i*+*s*.

The three different analytical reading processes (cf. pp. 29—32 above) might be classified as "active" or "passive". Adjunction is an active process, whereas deletion is a passive one. Substitution, which may be seen as a combination of deletion and adjunction, has one passive and one active component. When reading *kommer* on the base of the previously learnt *komma* and the dependent morpheme -*er* (abstracted from earlier patterns) the morpheme -*a* is deleted and -*er* is adjuncted. The morpheme -*a* then belongs to the passive part of the substitution, -*er* to the active part.

It seems quite evident that adjunction and the "active" part of the substitution are more difficult and require more skill than do deletion and the "passive" part of the substitution.

Now, if we consider the 23 dependent morphemes above—in what reading processes are they introduced for the first time?

The morphemes occurring in analytical readings in M a r c h are -*a*, -*ar*, -*de*, -*en*, -*na* and -*s*. During that month three of them occur only in deletions (-*s* 2.3, -*a* 4.3 and -*ar* 23.3), two occur in adjunctions (-*en* 1.3 and -*na* 25.3), and one (-*de* 25.3) in the active part of a substitution. Of the last three, however, -*en* and -*de* are graphically identical with very frequent independent morphemes already introduced in the first book in December: the indefinite article *en* and the pronoun third person plural *de*. Thus -*en* and -*de* need not have been extracted from earlier patterns, and on that account they are in a unique position compared with the other dependent morphemes which have no such homographs among the independent morphemes. The only remaining "truly" dependent morpheme used actively in March is -*na*, and it does not occur until the 25th of March, whereas the deletions of -*s* and -*a* are made as early as the beginning of that month (compare above). During the following months, however, the dependent morphemes, introduced only in passive processes in March, figure in all the analytical processes: -*a* in several deletions, ad-

junctions and substitutions during all the following months, *-ar* in deletions, adjunctions and substitutions from the month of May, *-s* in adjunctions from May onwards and also in "active" substitutions from the
month of June.

The dependent morphemes introduced in analytical reading processes
in April, *-an*, *-er*, *-or* and *-r*, are all first used in deletions or in the passive
part of substitutions. Only one of them, *-r*, is also used "actively" in
April, but not until the 19th, after having been deleted on the 1st and
substituted on the 4th. From the month of May, *-er* and *-or* figure in "active" processes; the less frequent *-an*, however, does not do so until October (in the passive part of a substitution it is found once in July and
once in September).

From May on, however, the newly introduced dependent morphemes
all figure for the first time in active processes, with the exception of *-n*
which is deleted on the 6th of June but then used in an adjunction the day
after.

In May *-are*, *-e*, *-et*, *-ig*, *-ing* and *-t* are all introduced in adjunctions;
in June *-te* is introduced in an adjunction, *-ande* and *-d* in the active part
of a substitution. In July *-is* and *-it* and in October *-el* figure for the first
time, all in the active part of substitutions.

We thus see a very clear tendency. From March on dependent morphemes are being used in analytical processes. As March is the very first month
of analytical reading, it is quite evident that the processes themselves
are very difficult to the reader. Thus—to begin with—only those dependent morphemes which have homographs among the independent
morphemes figure in the active processes. The others figure in passive
processes only. The handling of dependent morphemes in analytical readings seems still to be hard work in April, as dependent morphemes are
always introduced in passive processes. From May onward, however,
not only morphemes previously introduced figure in the active
processes; all "new" morphemes occur directly in adjunctions and in the
active part of substitutions. The introductory stage of two months, when
the analytical reading process and the handling of dependent morphemes
is performed with great effort, is followed from the month of May
by a period of greater skill. This greater skill is also evident from the fact
that in May for the first time we find correct readings of new words
containing dependent morphemes without immediate patterns
in earlier reading material:[61] morphemes which are themselves

---

[61] *-ig* and *-ing* in May, *-ande* and *-d* in June, *-is* in July (compare above p. 65).

read with the help of analytical processes, such as *-ing* (from *ingen* minus *-en;* comp. p. 65).

B. Analytical readings containing strings of dependent morphemes

The reader's growing skill also manifests itself in an ability to cope with more and more complicated structures. In March only single dependent morphemes are used in the analytical readings. But from April strings of morphemes also appear, as when the new *bilarna* is read correctly because the reading material already known contains *bil* and pairs like *boll — bollar, klapp — klappar, ankor — ankorna, blommor — blommorna* etc. from which the dependent morphemes *-ar* and *-na* might be drawn.[62]

The example given above shows the process of adjunction, where two dependent morphemes take part, forming a string of such morphemes. From April on we have also examples where strings of morphemes are deleted or substituted. An instance of deletion occurs when *studs* is read because the earlier reading material contains *studsade* and the morphemes *-a* and *-de* in word pairs like *sov — sova, fråga — frågade.*

A result of substitution is *mammorna* (in May) on the base of *mamma* (*-a* having been replaced by *-orna*) and the morphemes *-or* and *-na* drawn from word pairs lika *flicka — flickor, ankor — ankorna, blommor — blommorna* etc.

As time passes on, more and more strings of dependent morphemes are introduced into the analytical readings. A table of these strings and their occurrence during the different months, with the first appearance of every string denoted by an italicized *x*, looks like this:

TABLE XIII.

	April	May	June	July	Sept.	Oct.
-a-de	*x*		x	x	x	x
-a-de-s				*x*		
-an-de-s			*x*			
-ar-na	*x*	x		x	x	x
-are-n				*x*		

[62] Compare the reading *pengarna* in March, where the result of the reading is a word form containing two dependent morphemes, but where the adjunction is that of the earlier *pengar* + the morpheme *-na.*

	April	May	June	July	Sept.	Oct.
-de-s			x			
-en-s				x	x	
-er-na	x					x
-ing-ar				x		
-lig-a	x					
-lig-ast						x
-lig-en						x
-lig-t				x		
-na-de				x		
-na-r						x
-na-s				x		
-ning-en			x		x	
-ning-s						x
-or-na	x	x				x
-r-na			x			
-st-e					x	

The table shows that more and more strings of morphemes are handled in the analytical processes. In April there are only two, in May four, in June four, and during July, September and October eight each month. The number of newly introduced strings increases from two in April to six in July. Both in September and October four new strings are handled.

Now, what are the patterns for each one of these strings of dependent morphemes when they first appear in analytical readings?

Three cases occur:

1. There may be patterns for the whole string of morphemes, as when *somliga* (16.5) is read as an adjunction of *som* and *-liga*—where the combination *-lig-a* might be drawn from *vän — vänliga*, which words occur already in March. When there are patterns for the whole string, the analytical reading is mainly of the same kind as where a simple morpheme is implied.

2. The process is more complicated, however, when there are patterns only for each one of the morphemes in the string, i.e. the reader must herself combine the parts. This is the case when *bilderna* (22.5) is read as an adjunction of the earlier learnt *bild*, *-er*, mastered in April, and *-na* mastered in March.

3. We have a slightly more complicated case when one or more parts in the string has no immediate patterns but must be produced by means of analytical readings. This happens when, in September, *jätteroligt* is

read as an adjunction, where *-lig* must be formed on the base of the already mastered *-liga* by deleting *-a*.

Looking again at the 11 strings of morphemes listed above, the material shows that six of them have patterns for the whole combination as they first appear, twelve have patterns only for the parts, and in three cases one of the morphemes in the string is itself formed by using one of the analytical processes.

TABLE XIV.

	Patterns for whole string	Patterns for parts	One part of the string is the result of analytical reading
April	-a-de	-ar-na	
May	-lig-a, -or-na	-er-na	
June		-de-s, -an-de-s	
July	-are-n, -en-s	-a-de-s, -ing-ar, -ning-en, -r-na	
Sept.	-st-e	-na-de, -na-s	-lig-t
Oct.		-na-r, -ning-s	-lig-ast, -lig-en

Looking at the table above we see a certain tendency towards greater skill in handling strings of dependent morphemes in analytical readings. In April there are only two such strings, one of which has patterns for the whole string. In May two of the three newly introduced strings of dependent morphemes have patterns for the totality. But from June on there is a certain dominance of strings with patterns only for the parts. In September and October we find instances of strings of dependent morphemes where one of the parts is itself the result of analytical reading.

There are some correct analytical readings where the reader has worked with word endings which graphically resemble strings of morphemes, but where one or more of the parts of the string is no morpheme. In October the correct reading *tap-e-t-er* is made as an adjunction of *tap* (probably deleted from the earlier *tappar*) and *e+t+er*, where *-er* is a morpheme, but where *-e* and *-t* only graphically resemble morphemes. A string like *-e-t-er* we call a false string. Apart from *-e-t-er*, in October, we find the following false strings in the material: *-or(r)-ar-na* (*ek* is read correctly in April on the base of the earlier learnt *ek-orrarna*; this is a deletion made possible by the fact that the girl has learnt the morphemes *-or*, *-ar* and *-na* in her earlier reading material), *-n-an*, *-n-or* and *-t-it* (May), *-n-et*, *-r-a* and *-r-ade* (June), *-r-e* and *-t-ig* (July), *-n-en* and *-r-or* (Sept.), *-a-s*, *-ra-r-e*, *-s-ar*, *-s-na*, *-t-en*, *-t-ligen* and *-t-ligt* (Oct.).[62a]

Of these 19 false strings 14 have been put together from, or identified on the base of, parts which were already mastered before the string appeared. Three of them, *-n-en*, *-n-or* and *-t-it*—all appearing in May— have only patterns for one of the parts: the single dependent *-n* is not used in analytical readings until June, *-it* not until July, but there are patterns for *-n* as early as March and for *-it* in April. Two of the 19 strings, *-t-ligen* and *-t-ligt*—both appearing in October—consist of parts which are the result of analytical readings (cf p. 69 f.).

Our investigation of the false strings seems to confirm the earlier results. March and April are months where the analytical readings of dependent morphemes afford a certain difficulty. Only one string is involved during this period: *-or(r)-ar-na* on the last of April in a deletion, i.e. a "passive" type. All the parts in the string are already mastered. During the second half of May—the month when the skill in handling morphemes suddenly increases—the three strings appear where there are only patterns for one of the parts: *-n-en*, *-n-or* and *-t-it*. Strings containing parts which are themselves the result of analytical readings do not occur until October.

C. Unsuccessful readings

Among the analytical readings during the period from the first of April to the end of October where dependent morphemes are implied there are many unsuccessful readings.

TABLE XV. Analytical readings where dependent morphemes are involved

	April	May	June	July	Sept.	Oct.
Total number of readings	25	71	72	69	77	72
Correct	56 %	63 %	65 %	48 %	77 %	75 %
Wrong	44 %	37 %	35 %	52 %	23 %	25 %
Wrong where a dependent morpheme is involved in the mistake	12 %	11 %	17 %	13 %	5 %	7 %

[62a] These readings represent an intermediate stage: they might as well have been treated among the graphematic readings in Chapter Eight, as readings of graphemes which are homographic with dependent morphemes and which occur at the ends of words (compare p. 78). For the purpose of comparison with real morphematic readings, however, I have preferred to account for them here.

In the table above we see that—with the exception of July, when more than half of the analytical readings containing dependent morphemes are wrong—the mistakes become fewer and fewer. While in April slightly less than half of these readings are wrong, in September and October only one fourth are wrong.

Now, what sorts of mistakes are made? Looking at the misreadings we find that as a rule the dependent morphemes are correctly handled. Only in about a third to a quarter of the misreadings is a dependent morpheme involved in the mistake. The sole exception is June, when a dependent morpheme is incorrectly handled in half of the incorrect analytical readings containing such morphemes.

Let us take a few examples. When *gröten* is read *grönen*, the dependent morpheme *-en* is correctly identified, but the base *gröt* is wrongly supposed to be *grön*, i.e. we get an adjunction of the misidentification *grön* and *-en*. In the same way *lagat* is read *talat* on the base of *talade* and *-t*, where the substitution of the morpheme *-de* for the morpheme *-t* is quite correctly made, but where *laga* is wrongly supposed to be *tala*, i.e. is misidentified.

Mistakes due to wrong handling of dependent morphemes are, among others, *klappade* read as *klappande* (on the base of *klappar*) or *fortare* read as *fortade* (on the base of *fort*). In the examples where the dependent morpheme is involved in the mistake other parts of the word read may also be wrong, as when *råkade* is read *åkte* (on the base of *åker*).

Our next question is: What dependent morphemes are involved in mistakes? A problematic dependent morpheme is *-ade*. In March *hittade* is read *hittde*. The morpheme *-ade* is not recognized but part of it, *-de*, is observed. In April, however, we may observe a quite opposite tendency: all the mistakes in April involving dependent morphemes are of a kind where *-ade* is read instead of another morpheme: *-a*, *-are* and *-de* are all supposed to be *-ade*. The reason for this seems to be that in March the first book in the past tense is presented. There we find *skutt* twice and *skuttade*—from which *-ade* might be extracted—eight times. Moreover the book is highly redundant in style with many repetitions; the following sentence appears seven times: "Så *skuttade* den lilla geten vidare uppför kullen. Den *nosade* på det mjuka gräset och *smakade* på de gröna stråna, men den var inte glad". This overdose of forms ending in *-ade* not only guarantees correct readings of words in *-ade* but also seems to predispose the reader to change morphemes containing one or more of the graphemes *a*, *d* and *e* into *-ade*: *-a*, *-de* and *-are* are all supposed to be *-ade*.

The problem with -*ade* remains. In June the readings where -*ade* is involved are more often right than wrong, but still we find one instance where -*de* is supposed to be -*ade*, and another where -*ade* is mistaken for -*de*. In July we find the last case where -*de* and -*ade* are confused. It is to be observed, however, that from June onward -*ade* is only mixed up with -*de*, that is with a morpheme which also contains the strongly "determining" or "dominating" letter *d*.[63] A higher degree of similarity has thus become necessary to cause a misidentification.

Some of the misreadings of dependent morphemes in May are of a more incidental character, as when -*igt* is once read -*ig*, -*na* is read -*nan*, and -*it* is read -*tit*. The rest of the misreadings, however, are more interesting, as they tell us something about the conflict between similar morphemes. These similar morphemes are the strings -*arna*, -*erna* and -*orna*. All three strings have strong patterns as early as February.

In April a correct adjunction is made with the help of -*arna*; on the 17th of May we find -*arna* in a correct substitution: *pojkarna* read on the basis of *pojke*. As for -*orna* the reader falls short of reading *tofflorna* on the second of May (it becomes *telefonerna*). But on the 16th of May we find the correct substitution -*a*/-*orna* when *mammorna* is read on the basis of *mamma*.

On the 23rd, however, we find that *plaska* is read *pallarna*. This seems to show the same tendency as when -*ade* is read instead of -*a*, -*are* and -*de*. The string -*arna* has been met with in many words of the material and it has also been succesfully used in new readings. Probably such readings of strings have been received with great applause as they are more complicated than the readings of simple morphemes. So the reader tends to read -*arna* even when she is confronted with an ending like -*a* in *plaska*!

On the 22nd of May the word *bilderna* is shown to the girl. She first mistakes -*erna* for -*arna*, but on being asked to reread the word, she succeeds with some difficulty.

The string -*arna* affords some difficulty also in June and July. In June -*arna* is mistaken for -*ar*, in July -*na* is once supposed to be -*arna*. In September and October we find only correct readings with -*arna*. A new analytical reading with -*erna* does not, however, turn up until October, and then it is correct. As for -*orna* it is correctly used from the end of May onward.

The confusion of -*a* and -*arna*, -*erna* and -*arna*, -*na* and -*arna*, -*arna* and -*ar*, might also be seen against the background of Goldschei-

---

[63] Compare pp. 24 and 74.

der's and Müller's theory about "indifferent letters" as opposed to "determining letters" (Zeitler's and Messmer's "dominating letters"), as *a, e, n* and *r* are all indifferent letters and thus of less importance in the characterization of the form of the word.[64]

Apart from *-ade* and *-arna,* which have been treated above, the problematic morphemes in June are *-te* and *-ande.* The morpheme *-te* is used for the first time in an analytical reading, when *visste* is read correctly on the basis of *visslar* (7.6). On the same day, however, *-te* is used twice incorrectly: *råkade* is read *åkte* (on the basis of *åker*) and *stöta* is read *högte* (on the basis of *höga*). In the second misreading *-ta* is probably mistaken for *-te.* But in the first misreading there seem to be other reasons than the visual mistake *-ade—-te.* On seeing *råkade* the reader remembers *åker* and realizes that *-er* should be substituted for another ending. The morpheme *-ade* in *råkade* is already seen to be a problematic one (compare above); it is very often mistaken for *-de.* Granted that the reader observes *-de* and adds this to *åk, -de* must here for phonetical reasons be pronounced as *-te.* This reading is reinforced by the fact that it gives a verbal form well known to the reader in her spoken language; it is in accordance with her knowledge of the grammatical structure of Swedish.

Other readings with *-te* do not occur until September and October, and these are correct.

The first word ending in *-ande* occurs in the reading material during February: *tjattrande.* Not until June, however, are there clear patterns from which *-ande* may be extracted. *Springande,* which is presented on the 8th of June before these patterns occur, is (on the basis of *springer*) read *springland: -ande* is mistaken for *-land.* When *springande* has been learnt the first pattern for correct readings of words ending in *-ande* exists. Already the next day such a correct reading is made: *flytande* is read on the basis of *flyter* and *-ande.*

But the morpheme *-ade* is very similar to *-ande,* and to this graphical similarity is added the fact that both endings give grammatically correct forms to the same verbs. On the very same day as *-ande* is used correctly in *flytande* (9.6), *klappade* is supposed to be *klappande* (on the basis of *klappar*).

The confusion *-ande—-ade* remains. In both July and September *-ande* is mistaken for *-ade.* The two remaining readings with *-ande*—one a substitution in September and one an adjunction in October—are both correct.

[64] See Huey, pp. 79, 87 and 91.

The treatment of the string -*ningen* is also of considerable interest. The reading material presented in May contains the first word ending in -*ningen*: *bäddningen*. In June the dependent morpheme -*n* is being used in analytical readings, but patterns for these readings exist since as early as March. Moreover the word *ingen* is well known since the beginning of the year. Thus it is possible for the reader both to distinguish -*ningen* in *bäddningen* and to analyse it into *n*+*ingen*. When the word *sluttningen* is presented on the 5th of July it is read *skuttningen*, on the basis of *skuttade* and -*ningen*: the string -*ningen* is mastered. When, however, *landshövdingen* is presented on the 25th of July, this word too is thought to end in -*ningen*: it is read *landshövningen* (probably on the basis of Eng*land*, -*s*, be*höv*de and -*ningen*, a rather complicated operation). In the same way, *återigen* is read as *återningen* at the end of July, on the basis of *åter* and -*ningen*. From this we see that, although both *ingen* and *igen* frequently occur as independent morphemes (words) in the reading material, the reader is changing them to -*ningen*. The reason might be that the morphematic structure of written Swedish as the reader knows it compels her to put -*ningen* at the end of a word, and not -*ingen* or -*igen*. It is to be observed that the reading material does not contain any word ending in -*ingen*, only words ending in -*ing* and -*ingar*. Thus there are only patterns for the string -*ningen*. Compare the fact that in October *parkeringsplatser* is read as *parkningsplatser*.

There are seven more misreadings of morphemes in the material, four in September and three in October. They are all of an incidental character, but a few might be of a certain interest, as they show that the structure of the written language as known by the girl guides her choice of morphemes. When *bukett* is presented on the 6th of September it is read *buske*. The earlier reading material contains *buskar*; thus the reader remembers *buskar*, supposing that the two bases *buk*- and *busk*- are identical, but instead of substituting -*ar* with -*ett*, which is well known as an indefinite article, she substitutes -*ar* with -*e*, which is only part of the ending -*ett*. It cannot be that she is unable to distinguish -*ett*. The reason must be that her knowledge of morphematic structures compels her to choose -*e* as it gives the "correct" word *buske*. The foreign morpheme -*ett* is not yet part of her grammar. The same tendency is shown when *kullerbyttor* (14.9.) is read in the following way: "*kulle . . . kullar . . . bytt-or*". Earlier reading material contains *kullen*. The beginning of *kullerbyttor* is first analysed as *kullen* minus -*n*. Then she suddenly sees that an -*r* follows, but instead of adding this -*r*, which she is technically able to do (adjunctions with -*r* occur from April and on), she substitutes *kulle — kullar* to get a morphematically correct form—the combination *kull-er* violates her grammar.

Structural reasons probably underlie the choice of endings in the incorrect reading of *mångare* instead of *månader* (14.9), and of *omlysa* instead of *ompysslad* (14.9). The word *månader* is analysed into the earlier known *många*+ending. As *-er* is one of the best mastered endings in the analytical readings, it is impossible that the girl should fail to distinguish at least *-er*. But *många-d-er* or *många-er* are structurally impossible. Thus *mångare* is chosen. The reading *omlysa* is made on the basis of *om*+*lyste*: *ompyssl-* is supposed to be *om*+*lys-*; then *-a* is chosen from the ending *-ad* in *ompysslad* to give the structurally plausible form *omlysa*.

Chapter Eight
Third period (April 1ˢᵗ 1966—Oct. 31ˢᵗ 1966): Analytical readings of graphemes

In March, after six months of accumulating memorized reading material where the word had been the presented entity, a period of active reading began. The new words presented were compared with the already known reading material as it was memorized by the reader. This confrontation was carried out in two ways. Either the new words presented and the memorized words were treated as entities—if a new word was then wrongly supposed to be a previously learnt word, the result was a misidentification—or the new word and/or previously learnt words were analyzed into parts and compared. Then the reading was performed by manipulations with these parts. Morphemes constitute the first type of parts observed in this way.

The reasons why the morphemes—especially the dependent ones—and not the graphemes are the most easily observed parts of the word seem quite obvious. First, the fact that the morpheme is a semantic entity supports the tendency to segmenting into morphemes rather than into graphemes. Secondly, there is no complete parallelism between the graphematic and the phonematic systems of the Swedish language. The syngraphemes *s*, *c* and *z* all three correspond to the phoneme /s/; *x* corresponds to a combination of phonemes /ks/ etc. The phoneme /ɧ/ has got about 40 graphematic representations in Swedish.[65] With the morphemes, however, especially the dependent flexional ones, there is normally complete correspondence between the graphematic and the phonematic forms: a given graphematic entity or sequence of graphemes corresponds to a phonematic entity or sequence of phonemes.[66]

The graphotactic relations are numerous and complicated. But the position of a certain dependent morpheme is always given; as to flexional morphemes they always occur at the ends of words, singly or in combinations with other dependent morphemes, whose interposi-

---

[65] See Sture Allén, "*Förhållandet mellan skrift och tal*".

[66] There are exceptions, as when the word-forming morpheme which is pronounced [ɧ o :n] is graphically represented by -*tion* in some words (e.g. *inspektion*) and by -*sion* in others (e.g. *explosion*).

tions are governed by rigid rules. The genitive morpheme -*s* is always put at the end of a noun (pappa-*s*), if the noun is put in its definite form, the morpheme denoting definiteness precedes the genitive morpheme (pappa-*n*-s), and if you have the plural form of the noun, the plural morpheme precedes the definite morpheme (papp-*or*-na-s)[67].

The dependent morpheme—or the string of dependent morphemes—is joined to independent morphemes as bases. These bases very often have the same graphic form as the corresponding single words, which simplifies the identification of the morphemes to the reader: compare *sked — sked-en, flicka — flicka-n, barn — barn-s*.

We have observed that the analytical readings start in March with simple morphemes; strings of morphemes do not occur until April, and are only gradually mastered (see p. 68 f.). But we also observed that in April there are instances of readings of "false" morphemes (p. 64). The word *fönsterruta* is read as *fönster+ut+a*, where the identification of the *a* is made possible by the fact that -*a* has previously been learnt as a dependent morpheme and that -*a* in *fönsterruta* takes the same position as the dependent morpheme -*a* in *grön-a, läs-a* etc. Readings of "false" morphemes in combinations with real morphemes at the end of words have also been noted, the so called "false strings" (p. 70 f.). With the "false" morphemes the reader is not supported by the semantic component. To make the reading *fönsterruta* she must depend solely on her knowledge of grapho-phonematic correspondences in certain positions: that, for instance, an -*a* corresponds to an /-a/. The reading of the -*a* in this example might be supported by the morphematic position of the -*a*. All readings of this kind have therefore been treated as morphematic readings. From here it is a short step, however, to the realization that an -*s* corresponds to an /s/ in any position. When this is realized the reader has left the morphematic level and has entered the graphematic reading level. A still more advanced stage has been reached when the reader makes analytical readings using graphemes which are not homographic with morphemes, such as *b, k, l, m*.

A. Three early graphematic readings

During the month of March all analytical readings are confined to the morphematic level. In April, however, we find not only the first readings of "false" morphemes but also three analytical readings where the graphematic level is touched:

[67] Compare Bengt Sigurd, *Språkstruktur*, p. 48 f.

1. *grinden* (1.4) is first read as *grisden* /gri : sden/ (morphematic reading with misidentification of the first part of the word) but then it is corrected to *grinden* /grinden/;
2. *blek* (20.4) is read correctly;
3. *morgonen* (30.4) is read correctly /mɔjgɔnen/.

Let us first consider the correction /gri:sden/—/grinden/. When /gri:s/ is corrected to /grin/ the long vowel /i:/ is changed to the short one /i/, which shows that we have a substitution /i:s/ in/. How is this substitution made?

When the word *grinden* is presented, it is first wrongly supposed to be *gris+den*. In the already known word *gris* the reader is able to identify *i* corresponding to the sound /i:/ and *s* corresponding to the sound /s/, as both frequently occur as morphemes: *i* as a preposition, *-s* as the Swedish genitive morpheme. Moreover, *-s* in *gris* takes the position typical of the genitive morpheme *-s*. If the reader is able to identify *i + s* /i: + s/ she must also be aware of the fact that the string *gr* in *gris* corresponds to /gr/ in /gri:s/, because she knows the correspondence *gris* /gri:s/. Then, having another look at *grinden* she will be able to delete /i:s/ from her first wrong reading form /gri:sden/, reading /gr . . ./, and then she will add *in* (which is already well known as an independent morpheme) to the beginning *gr*, reading /grin-den/. All the elements involved in this analytical reading are morphematic except the sequence *gr*. The adjunction of *gr+in* might thus be considered a graphematic reading. But the identification of *gr* is made on the base of already well-known morphemes.

As regards the reading *morgonen* /mɔj-gɔn-en/, *mor* is taken from *mormor*, pronounced /mɔjmɔj/, and *-en* is the well-known dependent morpheme. The only pattern for *-gon-* is *ögon* /ø:gɔn/. The abstraction of *-gon* from *ögon* is possible because the correspondence *ö* /ø:/ has been learnt from the alphabet (cf. pp. 13 and 83): in reciting the Swedish alphabet you pronounce the graphic sign *ö* as /ø:/. Thus the reader must also be aware that the written sequence *gon* corresponds to the sounds /gɔn/, and she then can read *morgonen* by adding *mor+gon+en*. The reading of *gon* might be characterized as a reading of a graphematic string which is a syllable but not a morpheme.

Grinden and *morgonen* thus illustrate partly graphematical readings of non-morphematic strings of graphemes, where the non-morphematic elements taking part in the processes are identified on the basis of earlier learnt morphemes or letters of the alphabet.

The reading *blek* /ble:k/ is more complicated. Two explanations of

the reading are possible. Looking at the word *blek* we see that it consists of
bl and *ek*, the last sequence being part of earlier reading material in the
word *ekorrarna*. As *ek* ends the word, the sectioning *bl+ek* seems quite
natural. The beginning *bl-* is easily identified by the reader on the basis
of the previously learnt words: *blommor, blåser* (Feb.), *bland, blir* (March)
blåsa, blev (April). In *blåser, blåsa, blir* and *blev* the initial *bl-* is followed by
autographemes which in these words have the same quality as they
get during alphabetic recitation (long vowels). This helps the reader to
observe the grapho-phonematic correspondence *bl* /bl/ so that she is
herself able to read the combinations *ble . . ., bli . . ., blå . . .* when they
appear as the beginning of new words. Moreover, to make the reading
bl-ek the reader must first make the deletion *ek(orrarna)*. A reading which
involves fewer and less complicated operations is the addition of *b* to
the earlier learnt *lek*. This means that the reader must realize the grapho-
phonematic correspondence of the single grapheme *b* to the single phoneme /b/: that is, the explanation of *blek* as *b+lek* assumes a genuine
graphematic reading, the first one in the material. There are numerous
words in the earlier reading material from which the correspondence
b /b/ might be drawn (see p. 87 f.), and this process being the least complicated, we assume *b+lek* to be the explanation for the reading of *blek*.

B. Graphematic reading: a definition

From May on the graphematic readings become more frequent. Before
we go on to investigate these readings we had better answer the question:
When is a reading considered to be graphematic?

As was stated previously, every reading has been analysed and put in
relation to earlier learnt reading material. If a new word is wrongly
read as a word which is included in the old reading material, the reading
is classified as a misidentification. When making a misidentification of this kind, the reader treats the whole word presented as an
entity.

Instead of representing a whole word that is included in the old
material, the reading of a new presented word might be the result of a
manipulation with parts of words (dependent and/or independent
morphemes) which are included in this material. E.g. *vägar* is read correctly because the earlier reading material contains *väg* and word pairs
like *hatt — hattar, valp — valpar, dag — dagar, boll — bollar* etc. Such a
reading might of course also be wrong. In that case the parts which
make up the new reading may be the result of a misidentification, as

when *gröten* is read *grönen* on the basis of the earlier learnt *grön* and *-en*. The difference between such a reading and the misidentifications above is that in the case of *gröten* the new word presented has been analysed into parts which are mistaken for certain morphemes; it is an analytical morphematic reading.

If, however, it is not possible to explain a reading either as a misidentification or as the result of morphematic analysis and combination of morphemes, the reading might be the result of manipulations with graphemes.

A reading is, however, very seldom purely graphematic. As we have already seen from the examples *mor-gon-en* and *b-lek* above, the patterns in the earlier reading material might indicate that the readings consist of both previously learnt morphemes and graphemes added to each other. Often these morphemes are only homographs of morphemes, as *mor* in *morgonen* and *lek* in *blek*.

With *blek* there was some uncertainty about the explanation of the reading process, as the patterns allowed two interpretations. Either *blek* is a result of adjunction of *bl* and *ek* where *ek* is a result of the deletion *ek(orrarna)* or it is the result of the adjunction *b+lek*. The process *b+lek* seemed "easier", and so this explanation was preferred. It is very seldom, however, that we need be uncertain about the interpretation of a reading process. Often the girl's way of reading a new word gives a clear indication. Such revealing ways of reading are: misreadings, corrections, successive readings and so-called sectioning.

A misreading may often give us the clue to the reading process, as when *gråta* is read /grɔta/, with a short *å*-vowel, which shows that *-åta* has been mistaken for *åtta* (eight), part of the earlier reading material. Thus the reading process must be an adjunction of the grapheme string *gr-* and the independent morpheme (word) *åtta*.

Whether a reading is graphematic may be revealed by corrections, as in the case of *grisden — grinden* above. Or two or more successive readings might give us the clue. This is the case when *ägg* is read "*lägg ... ägg*": the earlier material contains *lägger*, from which the morpheme *-er* is first deleted. Then the grapheme *l* is taken away. Other examples are *länge* read "*hängde ... längde*" (*hängde* was part of the old reading material), *bur* read "*bu ... bur*" and *brum* "*rum ... brum*" (*bu* and *rum* being part of the previous reading material).

Another way of reading which reveals what parts are observed is sectioning. When *musikkår* is read /mɯːs-iː-k-spɔːr/ (the earlier material contains the words *mus, i* and *spår*), it is evident that *k* is added as a grapheme to the rest.

The sectioning is a most important criterion of graphematic reading. At the end of October *högre* is read /hø:-gr-e/ in spite of the fact that the earlier reading material contains both *höga* and *högar*, which would lead us to expect the morphematic substitution *hög/a, -re* or *hög/ar, -re*. In this case, however, /hø:-gr-e/ is considered to be a graphematic reading on account of the sectioning, although there do exist patterns for a morphematic reading. It is to be observed that not until October do such instances occur (see p. 97).

Sometimes the girl herself reveals, by comments on the reading material, that the patterns she uses are graphematic. The earliest example is from the 16th of May. On being presented with the earlier unknown *parken* the girl reads it correctly. I ask her: "How can you read that?" She answers: "I have had *marken* before." The process must thus be substitution: *m-* in *marken* is replaced by *p-* (about the patterns for this substitution, see p. 89).

To sum up, a reading is considered as graphematic:

1. if the way of reading or the reader's own comments give clear evidence that it is;
2. otherwise, when the structure of the word and the earlier reading material give evidence neither of a misidentification nor of a morphematic reading.

C. Grapho-phonematic correspondences in Swedish

After stating the principles for classifying graphematic readings we should have a look at the graphematic system of Swedish. According to Sture Allén there are 28 alphabetic graphemes in Swedish, 9 autographemes and 19 syngraphemes:

autographemes: a, e, i, o, u, y, å, ä, ö

syngraphemes: b, c, d, f, g, h, j, k,[68] l, m, n, p, r, s, t, v, w, x, z

The phonematic correspondences of these graphemes are as follows[69]:

a	/a:/	mat	or	/a/	matt
e	/e:/	vet	"	/e/	vett; året
				/ɛ/	berg

---

[68] Allén treats *q* as an allograph of *k*

[69] The phonematic symbols are those used by Claes-Christian Elert in "*Ljud och ord i svenskan*", 1970.

i	/i:/	vit	or	/i/	vitt
o	/ɷ:/	bo	"	/ɷ/	bott
	/ɔ:/	son, kol	"	/ɔ/	gott, komma, tretton
u	/ʉ:/	hus	"	/ʉ/	hund
y	/y:/	byt	"	/y/	bytt
å	/ɔ:/	gå	"	/ɔ/	gått
ä	/ɛ:/	säl; här	"	/ɛ/	vätt; kärr, märk
ö	/ø:/	hö; hör	"	/ø/	höst; förr, mörk
b	/b/	bok			
c	/s/	cykel	"	/k/	copyright or /ç/ cembalo
d	/d/	dag			
f	/f/	fat			
g	/g/	gata	"	/j/	ge, göra, berg or /ɧ/ gest, ingen-jör
h	/h/	häst			
j	/j/	ja	"	/ɧ/	juste
k	/k/	katt	"	/ç/	kyla, köpa
l	/l/	lag			
m	/m/	mala			
n	/n/	nu			
p	/p/	paket			
r	/r/	rad			
s	/s/	sal			
t	/t/	tal			
v	/v/	veta			
w	/v/	watt			
x	/ks/	yxa			
z	/s/	zebra			

All autographemes have at least two phonematic correspondences, one short and one long. Furthermore *o* has got two pairs of corresponding phonemes, /ɷ:, ɷ/ and /ɔ:, ɔ/. When reciting the Swedish alphabet, one always uses the corresponding long phonemes. All the correspondences between autographemes and long phonemes—except /ɔ:/ as a manifestation of *o*—are therefore known by the reader from the alphabet. The girl in this experiment masters the alphabet by the middle of March, 1966 (see p. 32).

As regards the correspondence between autographeme and short phoneme it should be observed that the phonematic distinction between short /e/ in *vett* and /ɛ/ in *vätt* does not exist in the girl's spoken Swedish;

both are pronounced /ɛ/.[70] In her language there are thus the grapho-
phonematic correspondences *e* /e:/ and /ɛ/, *ä* /ɛ:/ and /ɛ/.

Some of the correspondences between autographemes and short phonemes are known from dependent inflexional **morphemes** that occur
in the reading material before April:

a /a/ dependent morpheme in patterns of February;

e /ɛ/ dependent morpheme in patterns of March;

o /ɔ/ dependent morpheme -*or* with patterns in March minus dependent
   morpheme -*r* with patterns in December (deletion).

Added to these is:

i /i/ independent morpheme, preposition; when read in context it is
   almost always short with weak stress.

In the morphemes listed above the vowels have **weak** stress. As has
been shown by Elert in *"Ljud och ord i svenskan"* (p. 64), there is no phonematic distinction between [ɔ] and [ɒ] in weak position: you pronounce
-*kor* in *kyrkor* either [kɔr] or [k ɒr]. It is also to be observed that in reading
flickor, gator etc. the girl always uses a pronunciation where the quality
of the vowel is sometimes [ɔ], sometimes [ɒ], never [e], which is otherwise a common pronunciation in the spoken Swedish of Stockholm.

The correspondences between autographemes and phonemes which at
the beginning of April cannot be mastered by the girl on account of her
knowledge of dependent morphemes and of the alphabet, are thus:

o   /ɔ:/   son
o   /ɒ/   bott
u   /ɯ/   hund
y   /y/   bytt
å   /ɔ/   gått; kåsör, byrå.
ä   /ɛ/   vätt; kärr, märk.
ö   /ø/   höst; förr.

It should be noted that a free variation between [ɔ] and [ɒ] is possible
where /ɔ/ has weak stress, as in *kåsör* and *byrå*. These might be pronounced
either [kɔˈsœːr] and [ˈbyːrɔ] or [k ɒˈsœːr] and [ˈbyːr ɒ]; see Elert, p. 65.

As for the short vowels above, however, it is evident from the readings
that a knowledge of the correspondences between the autographemes and
the short vowel variants is not necessary. When presented with a new
word which she tries to read on the graphematic level, the girl often
starts by "sounding" the long vowel and afterwards adapts the pronunciation to that of the short vowel.

[70] Compare Elert, p. 62.

Ex. /ɯ/   *frukt* is first read /f-r-ɯ:-k-t/ and then the synthesis /frɯkt/ is made.

/y/   *yngsta* is´read first /y:n-g-s-ta/ then /yŋsta/. Two adaptations of phonemes are made /y:/ → /y/ and /n-g/ → /ŋ/.

/o/   *plommon* is read /p-l- o:-m-m-ɔ-n/, /pl om-ɔn/, /pl omɔn/.

/ɔ/ ´ *stången* is read /s-t-ɔ:-n-g-e-n/, /stɔŋen/.

/ɛ/   *mattläggare* is read /mat-lɛ:-gare/, /matlɛgare/.

/ø/   *plötsligt* is read /plø:tsl-i-g-t/, /pløtsligt/.

Also with autographemes whose short correspondences might have been learnt from dependent morphemes this adaptation might be used, as when *inomhus* is first read /i:-nɔ-m-hɯ:s/, then /inɔmhɯ:s/.

The synthesis and the adaptations are made possible by the girl's knowledge of spoken Swedish.[70a] When listening to herself making the first, graphematic reading, she associates what she hears with the corresponding spoken word and adapts her pronunciation in a second reading.

The ability to tackle the **autographemes** in graphematic readings thus seems to rest primarily on the knowledge of the correspondence between the autographemes and the long variants of the phonemes.

D. Graphematic readings of syngraphemes

Five of the **syngraphemes** and their phonematic correspondences are well known before April because they are homonymous with morphemes—or parts of morphemes—which have patterns in the early reading material. The syngraphemes *n, r, s* and *t* correspond to mor-

---

[70a] This knowledge might depend on knowledge of the alphabet. It might also be—and this seems to me the most plausible explanation—that the girl has become aware of the correspondence between the autographemes and their phonemes when reading, in the same way as she has become aware of the correspondences between the syngraphemes and their phonemes: by abstracting them from groups of learnt words or syllables forming "minimal pairs": *bara — bära, bara — vara — fara, bära — lära — nära; be—bi—bu—bo, be—se, bo—vi—ni, bu—du—nu, bo—ko—ro.* In that case the learning of the alphabet has only reinforced the knowledge of the correspondences between the autographemes and the long phonemes. Anyhow, the autographemes (vowels) being the centre of the syllable and so the most conspicuous part, it seems plausible that the correspondences between autographemes and vowel phonemes should have been learnt easily even without the reinforcement from reciting the alphabet.

Because of the uncertainty as to what role the alphabetic recitation might have played in the learning process, I have chosen to clarify the gradual development towards full reading ablity—i.e. realization of all grapho-phonematic corerspondences—by investigating the readings of **syngraphemes**.

phemes in the early reading material; *d* might have been extracted from *-de*, as both *-de* and *-e* are well known as early as March.[71]

Thus, there remain 14 syngraphemes which have no corresponding homographic morphemes: *b, c, f, g, h, j, k, l, m, p, v, w, x, z.*

A priori it seems very likely that a great many of the early graphematic readings comprise, on the one hand, graphemes which have homographic morphemes and, on the other hand, autographemes, whereas the 14 syngraphemes above would be more sparsely represented. An investigation gives the following result:

TABLE XVI. Graphematic readings

	May	June	July	Sept.	Oct.
Total	12	13	42	43	92
Only autographemes or graphemes with homographic morphemes	6	2	11	17	20
Only, or also, other graphemes	6	11	31	26	72

From this table it seems that graphematic readings comprising only autographemes or graphemes with homographic morphemes are relatively more common in May—the month when graphematic readings first occur to any great extent—and in September—after the summer holidays, when a certain disorientation has been noticed. The tendency is very weak, however.

Now, what about the graphemes without corresponding homographic morphemes and without support from the alphabet—when and where do these graphemes appear in graphematic readings?

Of the 14 syngraphemes without corresponding homographic morphemes (see above line 4) *w, x* and *z*[72] do not appear in graphematic readings during the period of April—October 1966. The remaining 11 syngraphemes appear as follows. (First appearance is italicized. If a grapheme during one month only occurs in passive processes—deleted or substituted—it has been put within parentheses.)

---

[71] The isolated morpheme *-d* does not appear in the reading material until June.
[72] It is to be noted that *w* is used in Swedish only in certain names and in the word *watt;* and *z* also has a very low frequency. As for *x*, it is treated under grapho-phonematic irregularities; see p. 112.

TABLE XVII.

April	May	June	July	Sept.	Oct.
	p	(p)	p	p	p
b	b	—	b	b	b
	m	—	m	m	m
			v	v	v
				f	f
	k[74]	k	k	k	k
g[73]			g	g	g
			j	j	j
		(h)	h	h	h
	l		l	l	l
					c

From the table above we see that more and more syngraphemes without homographic morphemes are used in graphematic readings: in April there are only *b* and *g*; then one or two further graphemes are added every month, until in October all 11 syngraphemes are used. It is to be observed that the syngraphemes with one or several phonematic correspondences are always read in the most "normal" way: *k* is read /k/, *g* /g/, *j* /j/ and *c* /s/.[75]

When a graphematic reading is made, this means that the reader has realized the "sound-value" of a grapheme or a sequence of graphemes, which is to say the grapho-phonematic correspondence in question. Such correspondences must be drawn from the reading material learnt earlier. By reading words beginning in *ba* ... /ba:/, *bo* ... /bɔ:/, *bu* ... /buː:/, *bå* ... /bɔ:/ etc. where the second element is an autographeme, the sound value of which is known from the reciting of the alphabet,[76] the specific sound-value of *b* is easily perceived. If we look at the first correct readings of syngraphemes (cf. the table above: *b* and *g* in April, *p*, *m* and *k* in May etc.) and examine earlier reading material, we will find that there are always such clear patterns in this material.

b. When *blek* is read in April, presumably as an adjunction of *b+lek*, the following combinations of initial *b* and a subsequent autographeme exist in the earlier reading material and might thus serve as patterns:

[73] Only in the combination *gr-*, see p. 88.
[74] Only in the combination *skr-*, see p. 89.
[75] Realization of the fact that one grapheme might have several phonematic correspondences and the perception of other grapho-phonematic irregularities is treated on p. 105 f.
[76] Compare above, p. 83 and 85 note 70 a.

ba . . . /ba:/, *be* . . . /be:/, *bi* . . . /bi:/, *bo* . . . /b ɷ:/, *bå* . . . /bɔ:/. Moreover, the initial combination of *b* +*l* is found in the following words, all learnt before the month of April: *bland, ibland, blommor, blir* and *blåser*. An adjunction of *b* +*lek* implies that the grapho-phonematic correspondence *b* /b/ must have been perceived. This is confirmed by a reading in May of *brum* as *b* +*rum*.

g. As for *g*, it is first read in the initial combination *gr* : *grinden*. There is clear evidence that the starting point for this reading was the word *gris*. Apart from this there are the following words in the reading material beginning in *gr*- which might serve to confirm the realization of the correspondence *gr* /gr/: *grannar, grinvarg, grodorna, gräset, gräshoppan, grön, gröna, grönt*. Patterns earlier than April from which the grapho-phonematic correspondence *g* /g/ might be drawn are *jag, dag* and *går*.

More graphematic readings of the sequence *gr* occur at the beginning of words in July and October and medially in October (*hö-gr-e*). The graphematic reading in July is a deletion of a final -*ga*. From January on the reading material contains a lot of words ending in -*ga* which might serve as patterns for the identification, especially adjectives ending in -*iga*. Before July we find: *duniga, hungriga, lurviga, skrangliga, trevliga, ulliga* (January), *ihåliga* (February), *flitiga, somliga* (May), *färdiga, ulliga* (June). Compare also *flyga* (January), *ligga* (February), *säga, fråga, skygga* (March), *laga, saga, höga* (June). Several graphematic readings of *g* before -*a* and -*ar* occur both with final and initial positions in September and October. In September *g* is also read graphematically before a final -*or*; patterns are here provided by *vågor* in July. In all these readings of *g* it is bound to a morpheme that begins with, or is, an autographeme, the whole reading is thus of a syllabic kind and it is not perfectly clear if the reader has grasped the grapho-phonematic correspondence *g* /g/ *per se.*

The first graphematic reading of *g* where it is evident that this correspondence is realized occurs in October when *gummihjul* is being read first *brummihjul*, then *gummahjul*, i.e. *br*- is being substituted by *g*.⁷⁷

p. In May an initial *p* is introduced in the reading *parken*, where the girl herself says that she knows how to read it, because she has learnt *marken*

---

⁷⁷ The reading *brummihjul* is an adjunction of the earlier learnt *brum* +*i* +*hjul*, where *brum* is a misidentification. That the second reading (*gummahjul*) is the result of a substitution *br*-/*g*- (and -*i*-/-*a*- to get a word that exists in spoken languge!) is evident from the fact that the word *gumma* is not contained in the earlier reading material.

earlier. Patterns for the *pa*-reading are numerous; we might mention only *pappa* which is learnt as early as December. The substitution is certainly one of *ma-/pa-* on the base of two of the best known words in the material: *mamma* (= *ma*+(m)*ma*) and *pappa* (= *pa*+(p)*pa*).

Of the five graphematic readings in June and July, four are *pa*-readings. But the fifth, appearing on the 18ᵗʰ of July, shows that the correspondence between an isolated *p* and /p/ must have been grasped by that time at least. Then *pippi* is read: "*klippa . . . pippa . . . pippi*", with two successive and correcting substitutions in the misidentification *klippa*. The first substitution must be one of *kl-/p-*, not *kli-/pi-*, as the patterns for the combination *pi* are extremely poor: only *pinne*, learnt in April; and the combination *kli* is only known from the word *klippa*.

m. The substitution of *m* for *p* in *marken — parken* is the earliest example of a graphematic reading where *m* is involved. Patterns which enable the reader to realize the correspondence *m* /m/ and thus to make the deletion (*m*)*arken*, are among others *mamma*, which occurs 21 times in the reading material before the end of May. An adjunction of *m* is also made in May: *måtid* (should be *måltid*). Direct patterns for an initial *må* cannot be found, though possibly *små* which is represented nine times from January to May might have served as a help. Otherwise this adjunction gives evidence that the correspondence *m* /m/ is clear to the reader.

k. This also is first used in graphematic readings in May, but only in the combination *skr-* (*skrapar*); patterns are *skrangliga, skrubba, skrubbar* and above all *skrek*, where the knowledge of the word *ek* has further simplified the identification of *skr*. In June and July *k* is used in graphematic readings in the final combinations *-ka* and *-kade*. There are numerous patterns for these combinations in the reading material up to the end of May: *baka, kaka, leka, lika, mjuka, torka, viska, smakade. Smakade* and *mjuka* occur seven times each, *leka* nine times.

In five of the six other graphematic readings in July, which contain *k*, *k* is tied to other graphemes: *-kar* and *-ken* in final position, *kr-* (before *a*) and *kl-* (before *i*) in initial position. There are strong patterns in the material for all these combinations of graphemes, and thus there is no clear evidence that the sound value of the isolated *k* has as yet been fully understood. In July, however, the reading *vitt* also appears, where *vitt* is read on the base of *kvitt* (a really well established word because read over and over again in the second book, where the little birds say *"kvitt, kvitt"*). The deletion of *k* shows that the correspondence *k* /k/ is clear to the reader.

h. In June *länge* is read *längde* on the basis of the earlier learnt *hängde;* i.e. as a substitution *h*/*ängde, l-.* The identification *h* /h/, which is necessary to make the deletion (*h*)*ängde* is made possible by words like *har, hel, heter, hit, hos, hus, hål, här, hö,* all learnt before the end of June.

l. In June the syngrapheme *l* is used in the final combinations *-la* and *-lar*, and in initial position before *ä* when *ägg* is read on the base of *lägg*, and *länge* supposed to be *längde* on the base of *hängde*. Patterns for the final combinations *-la* and *-lar* are numerous: *alla* (6), *Bella, gamla, gula* (3), *handla, hela* (2), *Ingela, lilla* (19), *snälla* (7), *bollar, cyklar, dalar, gillar, handlar, kelar, rullar* (14), *spelar* (12), *trillar*.

All these occur before June. Patterns for the combination *lä-* are found in *lägger* (3), *läggdags* and *lämnade;* moreover the sound value of an initial *l* before a vowel might have been realized through the learning earlier of words like *lakan, laga, lapar, lade* etc. Both the readings *"lägg ... ägg"* and *"hängde ... längde"* show that the correspondence *l* /l/ is evident to the girl.

v. In graphematic readings *v* is first used in July (four instances). In initial position it is used before *a* in *varken*, read on the basis of *marken*, where *m* has been replaced with a *v*. Patterns for the inital combination of *va-* are numerous: *vackert, vackra, varje, varann, vatten* etc. Then, too, *v* is used in the adjunctions *harve* /har-ve:/ (wrong for *havre*) and *ve*(*c*) +*kor* /ve:k ɔ:r/, that is in initial and final position before *-e*. Here the word *vet* (occurring seven times in the reading material before July) might have served as a pattern, *-t* being known as a dependent morpheme and simplifying the identification of *ve*. The identification of a final *-ve* is made easier by the previously learnt words *över, löven, kalven*, where *ve* is followed by *-n*, well known as a dependent morpheme. The reading *välta* (on the basis of the earlier learnt *tält*) where *v* is substituted for a *t*, has no direct patterns where an initial *vä-* corresponds to a /v/ with a short vowel. But apart from words already mentioned, numerous examples in earlier reading material would make possible the identification of the correspondence between *v* and /v/, which is necessary in order to make the graphematic reading *välta*. Such words are *av* (8), *var* (20), *vad* (10), *vi* (10), *vår* (4), *räv*, where *v* occurs exclusively in combination with autographemes and graphemes already known as dependent morphemes.

j. In July the word *sjön* is read as /j-øn/. The adjunction of the grapheme *j* and *ön* (from the previously learnt *önskar*) is facilitated by words learnt earlier—like *ja, jag* (60), *ju, ej, oj,* etc.—where a *j* in final or initial position immediately before or after an autographeme makes possible an identification of *j* /j/.

f. Not until September are graphematic readings with *f* performed. Then the word *faktiskt* is read as *faskitisa* (nonsense word). The adjunction *fa-* is facilitated by earlier learnt words like *fall, fanns, farbror, farbröder, fast, fasa,* where *fa-* occurs initially. Moreover an initial *f-* before autographemes in words like *fot, foten, fin, fina, fint, få, får* makes possible the identification of *f* /f/. That such an identification has really been made in September is shown by the reading of *veta* (as "*feta . . . veta*") on the 29th. On the 14th of October the reading of *frukt* as "*f-r-u-k-t . . . frukt*" gives the final evidence.

c. In October, at last the correspondence *c* /s/ is grasped, as is shown by the readings /sement/ for *cement* and /ruskel/ for *ruckel*. Patterns are *precis* (already in December) and, above all, *cykel, motorcykel, motorcyklar, cykla* and *cyklade.*

Thus the investigation made above shows that when a graphematic reading of a certain grapheme occurs for the first time there are always earlier learnt words where this grapheme occurs in a position (initially and/or finally in immediate combination with an autographeme) that makes possible the identification of the "normal" grapho-phonematic correspondence. We have also seen that very often the actual grapho-phonotactic structure of part of the word thus read has got patterns in earlier reading material; compare *parken — pappa, skra*par — *skra*ngliga, viss*lar* — bol*lar,* cyk*lar,* da*lar* etc.

If we look at all the graphematic readings during the April—October period we shall find that very often there are strong patterns in earlier reading material for exactly the grapho-phonotactic structure of the surroundings of the grapheme thus read. This tendency seems, however, to be weaker in the readings of September and October, which should indicate a growing reading skill where the occurrence of direct patterns is no longer necessary for the reader to produce a correct graphematic reading.

Let us take a few examples. 13 graphematic readings of k from May to September all have immediate patterns for the grapho-phono-tactic structure of the immediate environment of the k. We find k in the initial combinations *skr-, kr-, kl-, kv-, ka-, ko-,* in the final combinations *-ka, -kade, -kar, -ken,* and in the medial combinations *-ik-* and *-uk-.* In September, however, the reading /faskiti:sa/—wrong for *faktiskt*—and in October the reading /k-i:-lade/ for *kilade* show a complete know-ledge of the correspondence between k and /k/ without the support of surrounding graphemes. A k before an i being normally pronounced /ç/, there are no patterns for the correspondence *ki* /ki/. In the same way, the reading in October of *förarhytten* as /fø:rarhten/, where the *y* is over-looked, shows a sure knowledge of the correspondence *h* /h/.

The graphematic readings of l in the April—September period all have direct patterns for the surroundings of l in earlier reading material. We find the initial combinations *bl-, kl-, la-, lä-, lu-,* the final combina-tions *-la, -lar, -lå* and the medial combination *-el-.* In October, however, the readings /plø:tsl-i-g-t/ and /p-l-ʊ:-m-m-ɔ-n/ are not supported by any other words beginning in *plö-* /plø:-/ or *plo-* /plɔ:-/.

The graphematic readings do not only show an increasing certainty in the reader's knowledge of the grapho-phonematic correspondences; they also become more and more complicated.

In the graphematic readings in April, May and June only one of the eleven syngraphemes (or combination of syngraphemes, such as *gris*) is added to, or deleted from, other elements: ex. *b-*rum, *p-*arken etc.[78] In July there are two graphematic readings where two of the syngraphemes are implied: ex. *köttbullar* /jøt-*b*u:-*l*ar/, in September and October the readings where two such syngraphemes are implied are two and fourteen respectively, and even as many as three appear in September (one instance) and October (six instances): ex. *elektriker* /e*l*e-*k*t-r-i-*k*-er/, *plommon* /*p*-*l*-ʊ:-*m*-m-ɔ-n/.

The graphematic readings become more and more complicated also in the sense that the number of other elements implied in the reading process increases. In April, May and June no more than one or two ele-ments besides the syngrapheme are involved: ex. *brum* /b-*rum*/, *måltid* /mɔ:-*ti:d*/. In July 16 % of the graphematic readings are such that on an

---

[78] But this single syngrapheme may of course be combined with one of the auto-graphemes, or a morpheme, or a grapheme, or a combination of graphemes which is homographic with a morpheme; compare below.

average three other elements are involved; in September 31 % of the graphematic readings contain from three to six other elements (on an average four), and in October 53 % contain from three to seven other elements (on an average four). The more numerous the elements, the smaller the units.

Examples of graphematic readings in October which have a great many elements added are *diskbänkar* /di:-s-k-b-ɛ:-n-k-ar/, *plötsligt* /pl-ø:-t-s--l-i-g-t/, *korkmattor* /k ɔ:-r-k-ma-t-ɔ-r/ etc. In these readings the words are decoded more or less "letter by letter", and the readings thus show a high degree of certainty about the grapho-phonematic correspondences.

E. Double readings, synthesis and preference for graphematic readings. The first spelling

The development from reading of words as "totalities" to analytical reading which takes place during the months of March to October (first analytical readings of morphemes, then, gradually, also of graphemes), is reflected in a few "double readings" of words, where the first try is a misidentification—i.e. a reading of the word as a totality—or the result of a more superficial analysis, and the second try is the result of a very careful analysis.[78a]

The earliest example is from the second of May, when *sätta* is first assumed to be *berätta*, but is then read /sɛ:-ta:/ as an adjunction of *s*, known as a dependent morpheme, of the autographeme *ä* and of the word *ta*. The other examples are as follows:

	Words presented	First reading(s)	Second reading
July	korna	/knɔra/ (a deletion of -*n* from the earlier learnt *Knorran*)	/k ɔ:-r-na/
	sopades	/skɔrpades/ (adjunction of the earlier learnt *skorpa* and the morpheme string -*de-s*)	/s ɔ:p-a-des/
Sept.	tårna	/tɔ:rta/ (misidentification)	/tɔ:r-na/

[78a] This analysis may sometimes be wrong as in /hɛ:r-tig-t/ and /st-y:-ra/ below.

Words presented	First reading(s)	Second reading
härligt	/fɛ:rdiga/ (misidenti-fication)	/hɛ:r-tig-t/ (ad-junction of *här*, *t*,
	/fɛrj/ (misidentifica-tion)	and the morpheme string *ig-t*)
stygga	/ny:a/ (misidentifica-tion)	
	/fy:ra/ (misidentifica-tion)	/st-y:-ra/
alltihop	/alih ɒ:p/ (misidenti-fication)	/alt-i:-hɒ:p/
stek	/skre:k/ (misidenti-fication)	/st-e:k/
Oct. leda	/le:na/ (misidenti-fication)	
	/le:a/ (adjunction of *le* and -*a*)	/le:-da/
inomhus	/ge:nɔm -hɯ:s/ (adjunction of *genom* and *hus*)	/i:nɔ-m-hɯ:s, inɔmhɯ:s/
tapeter	/tablɛter/ (misidenti-fication)	/tap-e:t-er, tape:ter/

The second readings of the last two words contain two variants, the first one an analytical variant, the second one a s y n t h e s i s of this anal-ysis.

If there is no synthesis of a word read analytically, you could rightly claim that the word has not been read at all. Very often the synthesis follows naturally from the analytical reading: such is the case with the readings of *tårna*, *alltihop*, *stek* and *leda* above, but in other cases it is necessary to sum up the items of the analytical reading in an extra syn-thetical reading. This is specially true of complicated graphematic readings.

There are 28 instances in the material where the reader, after having made her analysis, sums it up in a correct synthetical reading. One example is from July, two are from September, and 25 are from Octo-ber. One of the two September readings and 19 of the 25 in October are partly made up of syngraphemes of the type described above, p. 86 f., that is, without homographic morphemes.
The examples are:

	Words presented	Analytical reading(s)	Synthesis
July	sådde	/sɔ:-de/	/sɔde/
Sept.	smådjur	/smɔ:-d-jɯ:r/	/smɔ:jɯ:r/
	likadant	/li:ka-da:-nt/	/li:kadant/
Oct.	frukt	/f-r-ɯ:-k-t/	/frʊkt/
	plommon	/p-l-ʊ:-m-m-ɔ-n/	/pl ʊm-ɔn, pl ʊmɔn/
	plötsligt	/plø:ts-l-i-g-t/	/pløtsligt/
	fortfarande	/f ʊrt-far-a-nde/	/f ʊ:rtfa:rande/
	tusen	/tu:-se:n/	/tu:sen/
	slutat	/sl . . . slɯ: . . . slɯ:t-at/	/slɯ:tat/
	kappor	/a:pɔr . . . k-a:pɔr/	/kapɔr/
	gammalt	/ga-m-a-lt/	/gamalt/
	sneda	/sn-e:-d-a/	/sne:da/
	trassligt	/tra-s-l-igt/	/trasligt/
	lager	/la:-g-e-r/	/la:ger/
	verkstäder	/vɛrk-s-t-e:-d-er/	/. . . st-ɛ:-der, vɛrkstɛ:der/
	vinda	/vin-da/	/vinda/
	cement	/se:-m-e-nt/	/sɛment/
	murare	/mɯ:-ra-re/	/mɯ:rare/
	ställningar	/stɛ-l-ni:-n-gar/	/stɛlniɲar/
	högre	/hø-gr-e/	/hø:gre/
	elektriska	/ele-k-t-r-i-s-k-a/	/e-le:-kt-ri-ska, elɛktriska/
	spisar	/spi-s-sar/	/spi:sar/
	slutligen	/slɯ:tli-g-en/	/slɯ:tligen/
	klistrade	/kl-i:-s-t-r-a-de/	/klistrade/
	tapeter	/tap-et-ter/	/tape:ter/
	mattläggare	/mat-lɛ:gare/	/matlɛgare/
	korkmattor	/k ʊ:rk-ma-t-ɔr/	/k ʊ:rkmatɔr/
	lägenheten	/lɛ:-g-e-n-he:ten/	/lɛ:genhe:ten/

In the readings of *cement* and *korkmattor* the results are not quite correct, the accent being wrong in /ˈsɛ mɛnt/ and the quantity of /ʊ/ incorrect in /kʊ:rkmatɔr/. The reason for this is evidently that the reader is unfamiliar with both words in spoken language. We have three other instances of wrong synthesis—all from October—where the words are

familiar to the reader in spoken language but where she nevertheless
fails to make a correct synthesis.

Word given	Analytical reading	Synthesis
Ursula	/ɯːr-s-ɯːː-la/	/ɯːsla/
grunden	/grɯːː-n-d-en/	/grɯːnden/
diskbänkar	/diːsk-bɛːː-n-k-ar/	/iːskbeŋkar/

In October we also have twelve analytical readings where the reader
has totally failed to make any sort of synthesis. The reasons here are quite
obvious. Either the underlying analysis is in some way deficient or inappropriate, or the analysis is made up of such a great number of small
units that the reader cannot cope with them. Deficient analysis is found in
the following two examples:

Word given	Analytical reading
förarhytten	/føːrar-h-ten/
hemresan	/hem-r-san/

In four examples the reader fails to make the synthesis because the
sectioning made in the analytical reading is inappropriate and mis-
leading.

Word given	Analytical reading	
egentligen	/eːgen-t-ligen/	(The word is wrongly supposed to contain *egen*.)
skjul	/sk-jɯːl/	(In these two examples the
skjulen	/sk-j-ɯːl-en/	graphic sequence *skj* corresponds to a single phoneme and must not be sectioned.)
ruckel	/rɯːː-s-k-e-l/	(The *ck* here corresponds to the phoneme /k/ and cannot be sectio-ned.)

In the following five examples the analysis is made up of such a
quantity of small entities that the reader falls short of gathering them
into a higher unit:

Word given	Analytical reading	
ansiktet	/a-n-s-ik-t-et/	
elektriker	/ele-ka/kt-r-ik-e-r/	(Here the selfcorrection ka/kt-also diminishes the possibili-ties of a synthesis.)

byggnadsställning	/by:g-nads-s-t-ɛ:-l-n-iŋ/
balkongdörrar	/ba-l-k-ɔŋ-dørar/
parkeringsplatser	/park-er-i-ŋs-platser/

Only in one case where the reader has failed to make a synthesis is there no obvious reason for this failure: when *stilig* is read as /st-i:-l-ig/ without any kind of summing up.

The development towards analytical reading on the graphematic level is clearly illustrated by the fact that during the three last days of October the reader overlooks in many cases a more simple way of reading a word—through analysis into morphemes—and makes a more complicated graphematic reading. This is true in the following seven cases:

Word given	Reading	Simpler way of reading that is not chosen.
gammalt	/ga-m-a-lt/	gam/la, -alt (substitution of -*alt* for -*la* in already well-known *gamla*)
högre	/hø:-gr-e/	hög/a, -re (substitution of -*re* for -*a* in already known *höga*)
bakåt	/ba:-k-ɔ:t/	bak-åt
slutligen	/slɯ:tli-g-en/	slut-lig-en
inomhus	/i:nɔ-m-hɯ:s/	in-om-hus
ställningar	/stɛ-l-ni:-n-gar/	ställ/er, -ningar (substituion of -*ningar* for -*er* in earlier learnt *ställer*)
elektriska	/ele-k-t-r-i-s-k-a/	elektri/ker, -ska (substitution of -*ska* for -*ker* in earlier learnt *elektriker*)

These examples show a preference for graphematic readings that clearly indicates a growing certainty as to the grapho-phonematic correspondences. It is to be observed that by the middle of October all autographemes and syngraphemes in the reading material, except for *w*, *x* and *z*, have been used in correct graphematic readings.

The final evidence, however, that the code has been broken and the child attained full reading ability was given on the 31st of December. Some weeks earlier I had told her a story in which the Nordic goddess Freja plays an important part. It may be noted that she had never seen the name *Freja* printed. On the 31st of December the girl asked me "Who do you think I am today? It begins with an *f*. . . (spelling in a loud voice) *f, r, e* . . . (almost silently, to herself) *fre* . . ., *frej* . . . (spelling again in a loud voice) *j, a.*"

This transforming of a word from the spoken language to the written, from phonemes to graphemes, which is the reversed process of graphematic reading, gives full evidence that the code has been broken by the child.

After a period of 14 months the child has, by observing, learning, storing, analysing and comparing written words, and through the processes of adjunction, deletion and substitution—first of morphemes and graphemes homographic with morphemes, then of non-morphematic graphemes—arrived at a knowledge of the grapho-phonematic correspondences that is a prerequisite for being able to decode any written message.

Chapter Nine
Capital letters. Double syngraphemes. Some grapho-phonematic irregularities

A. Capital letters

A child learning to read by the method described in this book is always presented with whole words, usually in small letters. Capital letters are used only in cases where the book from which the words are taken actually makes use of capitals. The following sentence: "He heard Bill moving SLOWLY", gives five reading cards, three of which have words containing capitals: *He*, *Bill* and *SLOWLY*.

Moreover, when learning the letters of the alphabet in the January—March period the child was presented with both capitals and small letters. Thus, theoretically, by the end of March, she knew that *a* was "a small ei" and *A* was "a big ei". The question is now: if the girl had been presented with a word in small letters and was later presented with the same word in capital letters—or the reverse—could she then "transform" from small letters to capitals—or the reverse—helped by her knowledge of the two alphabets? There are examples in the material from the middle of May and onwards. First we are going to look at the cases where only the initial letter is a capital in the previously given word (or the new word presented) and a small letter in the new word presented (or the previously given word).

	New word presented	Previously learnt word(s)	Reading[79]	Process
17.5	trampar	Tramp	trampar	Adjunction tramp+ar, T → t
1.7	Ångvälten	gång kvällen	gångkvällen	Adjunction of two misidentified parts, å → Å

[79] All the readings have been rendered in small letters.

	New word presented	Previously learnt word(s)	Reading	Process
2.7	korna	Knorran	knorra	Misidentification with deletion of -*n*, K → k
13.7	piller	Pillerill	piller	Deletion of -*ill*, P → p
20.7	Stortorget	stor	storet	Adjunction *stor*+*et*, s → S
25.7	Landshöv-dingen	land behövde etc.	lands-hövningen	Adjunction *land*+*s*+*höv*+ +*ning* (misidentified) +*en*, l → L
6.9	goda	God	goda	Adjunction *god*+*a*, G → g
30.9	Hjälp	hjälper	hjälp	Deletion of -*er* from *hjälper*, h → H
30.9	Kras	krasch	krasch	Misidentification, k → K

These examples show clearly that the "transformation" from small to capital letters, or vice versa, does not afford any problem when there is only an initial letter to be transformed. In three cases, however, the new word given is written all in capitals:

	New word presented	Previously learnt word(s)	Reading	Process
8.6	PLASK	plaska	—	—
8.6	KVACK	kvack	plack[80]	Deletion from (*t*)*ack*, guessing of the first part under influence of

---

[80] The word presented the minute before was *plask*.

New word presented	Previously learnt word(s)	Reading	Process
			the word presented the minute before, ack → ACK
26.9 KOSSAN	ost kostar etc.	1. osten	Adjunction *ost+en* of misidentified parts. os ... n → → OS ... N
		2. kostan	Substitution with misidentification *kosta/r, -n* kos ... an → KOS ... AN

These readings show that a series of letters might also be transformed, but that this seems to afford certain difficulties. PLASK is not identified at all, and KVACK is read "plack" although its correspondence in small letters—*kvack*—is well established.

The problem of capital letters does not seem to be solved until the girl has acquired a good knowledge of the grapho-phonematic correspondences. From October (12.10) to November (12.11) there are eight graphematic readings of new words with an initial capital: *Ursula, Paola, Tusen, Fröken, Per, Lotta, Lena, Jakob, Johanna* and *Jumbo*.[81] In November, finally, the girl succeeds in reading new words consisting only of capitals.

	Words	Readings
19.11	FIAS	/fi:-a-s/
19.11	FJÄRILAR	/fjɛ:r ... fjɛ:r-il-a-r ... fjɛ:rilar/
30.11	LINDGREN	/l-i:-n-d-g-r-e:-n/

It is to be observed that the word *fjärilarna* has been learnt earlier, but that this does not influence the girl's reading of FJÄRILAR; she makes the reading entirely as an addition of graphemes.

From this we see that successful readings of words containing more than

---

[81] In four of these readings, *Ursula, Paola, Jakob* and *Johanna*, the identification of the capitals might be due to the earlier learning of whole words: *Ur, Pappa, Ja* and *Jo*. In the rest of the cases there are pure graphematic readings of capitals.

one capital are attained only when the grapho-phonematic correspondences between the "small" graphemes and the phonemes are thoroughly mastered. Then this knowledge seems to be transferred to the corresponding capitals.[82]

B. The problem of double syngraphemes

In Swedish there is a phonematic distinction between the stressed long vowels and the stressed short ones: /ha:t/ means "hatred", /hat/ means "hat". In the written language this distinction is usually expressed by the number of syngraphemes following the autographeme representing the vowel: /ha:t/ is rendered *hat*, /hat/ is rendered *hatt*. In the same way *gata* corresponds to the spoken form /ga:ta/, whereas *gasta* corresponds to /gasta/.

How does the girl in this experiment become aware of this grapho-phonematic rule?

I have investigated such readings in the material where the correct rendering of the vowel quality is dependent on knowledge of this rule. I have concentrated on the cases where the vowel is followed by one consonant, not a combination of different consonants, and where the written form must thus contain a double syngrapheme after the autographeme to indicate a short vowel in the spoken form (the type *hatt*).

During the period April to October, 1966, 17 such readings have been noted, 12 of which are incorrect.

	wrong	correct
April	1	—
May	1	—
June	2	1
July	2	1
Sept.	3	—
Oct.	3	3

Examples of incorrect readings are: *hette* /he:te/ (from the earlier learnt *hete(r)*, April), *mätte* /mɛ:te/ (from the earlier learnt *mä+-te*, June), *hurra* /huɪ:ra/ (from the earlier learnt *hur+-a*, July), *hann* /ha:n/ (graphematic reading, October), *gråta* /grɔta/ (*gr+åtta*, grapheme string adjuncted to misidentification, October).

The examples of correct readings might indicate two stages: first an analytical reading is made without notice being paid to the syn-

[82] Capitals and small letters are recognized by the middle of March 1966; see above p. 32.

grapheme, then the vowel quantity is corrected. Three of the five correct readings during the period are of this type. Ex. *hålen* 1. /hɔlen/ (from the earlier learnt *håll/er, -en*), 2. /hɔ:len/ (June), *sådde* 1. /sɔ:-de/ (from the earlier learnt *så+de*), 2. /sɔde/ (July), *kappor* 1. /k-a:pɔr/ (from *k+apor*), 2. /kapɔr/ (Oct.).

The two other correct readings are from the end of October, when *matt-* in *mattläggare* and *flytt-* in *flyttkarlarna* are pronounced with the right vowel quantity.

Starting from December there are no longer any reading-cards. The girl is presented with the new books directly. From this period only the reading mistakes have been wholly recorded. Consequently the correct rendering of the vowel quantity in new words has only been noted if there are also some mistakes in the reading of these same words. Thus the reading /fama/ for *flamma* has been noted because the *l* is missing. Other readings noted are those of the type mentioned above, where the reading is made in two stages, the correct vowel quantity being assigned at the second stage.

As in the period April—October, 1966, the mistakes are of two kinds: either short quantity is assigned to a vowel whose autographeme stands before a simple syngrapheme, *klut* /klʊt/, or long quantity is assigned to a vowel whose autographeme stands before a double syngrapheme, *stött* /stø:t/. There are about half of each type, both during April—October, 1966, and during November, 1966—June, 1967. As regards the "two-stage readings", however, in the second period they occur almost exclusively with words that have simple syngraphemes. These words are first read as if the syngrapheme was a double one; then the vowel quantity is corrected:

lät	/lɛt/	/lɛ:t/
len	/lɛn/	/le:n/
släp	/slɛp/	/slɛ:p/
tam	/tam/	/ta:m/ etc.

14 out of 19 "two- stage readings" noted during the period November, 1966, to June, 1967, are of this kind.

The mistakes in rendering the right vowel quantity seem to have reached their maximum in November and December, 1966; 10 instances have been noted during each of these two months. In January there are seven mistakes. In February only two mistakes have been noted, in March one, in April three and in May one. From June, 1967, onwards no instances of incorrect renderings of vowel quality have been observed.

Thus we see that there is a successive decrease in mistakes from December to the end of May, which means that performance according to the rule is almost perfect after May. From this we might infer that the rule must become known some time during the period of December, 1966, to the end of May, 1967. An analysis of the correct readings might give some additional information about the gradual understanding of the rule, the growing competence of the reader.

Two correcting "two-stage readings" have been noted in November and one in December. Moreover the vowel-quantity was rendered spontaneously in a correct way in the new words *Herren* and *kagge*, both occurring in literature presented in December, 1966. This gives a hint that perhaps the rule was already being grasped by the end of 1966. In January no less than 18 correct readings have been noted, seven of which are two-stage readings. The following combinations of autographemes and syngraphemes are represented: *inn, ymm, ull, äll, äpp, ugg, igg, arr, iss, oss, äss; al, et, år*. I then decided to test the girl's competence by putting a question to her. Therefore, when on the 25ᵗʰ of January she read *snåren* as /snɔren/, I immediately said: "Only one *r*". She corrected what she had said to /snɔ:ren/. From this I conclude that she must have known the rule; otherwise she would not have been able to understand my correction.

The two-stage readings and the spontaneous correct readings of new words do not always give sure evidence as to knowledge of the rule of quantity, because the reader might have made an intuitive adaptation of her reading in accordance with her knowledge of spoken language: reading *len* as /lɛn/ or *lås* as /lɔs/ she does not recognize the words as words in spoken language and therefore changes to /le:n/ and /lɔ:s/, which are well known to her. In cases like *lät* 1. /lɛt/, 2. /lɛ:t/ or *släp* 1. /slɛp/, 2. /slɛ:p/, however, where both spoken forms exist as words in the Swedish language, and where the change is thus not necessary to get the meaning, the new pronunciation gives more sure evidence.

Still better evidence is given by a misreading at the middle of March: *storrengöring*, made up of *stor+ren+göring*, is wrongly sectioned into *storr+en* (indef. article) *+göring* and thus read /stɔr-ɛn-jø:riŋ/ with a short vowel in the first section. If the rule had not been known, the reading would have been /stɔ:r-ɛn-jøriŋ/. The fact that the reader assigns short quantity to the vowel corresponding to *o* because it is followed by a double syngrapheme—in spite of the fact that there is no word /stɔr/ in the Swedish language—gives sure evidence that the rule of quantity is part of the reader's linguistic equipment in March, 1967.

Thus we see signs that the rule of quantity is perhaps known as early as the end of 1966. It is with certainty part of the reader's linguistic equipment in February—March, 1967. Nevertheless, sporadic errors are made in March, April and May: there is a gap between competence and performance. After May, however, it seems that this gap has been bridged.

C. Grapho-phonematic irregularities

Like all languages written with an alphabet, Swedish does not have totally phonematic spelling. The discrepancies between the graphematic and the phonematic systems are principally due to the fact that s p e l l i n g is c o n s e r v a t i v e. Whereas the pronunciation of words has often gone through many changes, the spelling has to a great extent remained unchanged. Other reasons for discrepancies are that spelling forms might be taken over from other languages, or they might be purely conventional, like the spelling with *ch* in *och*, which was first introduced by the Swedish "New Testament" of 1526.[83]

The grapho-phonematic irregularities are principally of four kinds:
1. One phoneme may be represented by a string of graphemes, as when /ç/ is rendered *tj* or /j/ is rendered *dj*.
2. One grapheme may be represented by a string of phonemes. This is true of *x*, which is pronounced /ks/.
3. One phoneme is sometimes represented by different graphemes: /ç/ may be written *tj, kj, k, ch;* /j/ might be represented by *j, g, dj, gj, hj* and *lj.*
4. One grapheme may correspond to different phonemes, as when *g* might be pronounced /g/, /j/ or /ɧ/.

How does a child, presented with written language in the way characteristic of this experiment, cope with the problem that these irregularities afford?

To answer this question I have gone through the material as far as the end of 1968. From November of 1966, however, there are complete

[83] A full account on written languages is given by I. J. Gelb in *A Study of Writing* (1963).

notes only about incorrect readings, whereas correct readings have been noted incidentally. That means that the girl's competence has got to be judged by the absence of notes.

The following graphemes or strings of graphemes will be dealt with:

1. ck
2. ng
3. g, k
4. dj, gj, hj, lj
5. tj, kj
6. sk, sj, skj, sch, stj
7. x

ck. The graphematic string *ck* represents one phoneme /k/. But it also has the function of signalling a short vowel; instead of *kk* one writes *ck*. Presented with *ck*, the reader must thus be aware of two things in order to make a correct reading: first that *c* in this combination does not represent /s/ but /k/, secondly that as *c* here has the function of *k*, the preceding vowel should be short.

The first note about *ck* is from June, 1966, when the girl meets the word *stockarna*, then presented to her, with complete silence. In October and November, however, the girl has grasped the correspondence of *c* to /s/ and consequently makes the following incorrect readings: *ruckel* /rɯ:-s-k-e-l/ (29.10.66), *veckan* /ve:-s-kan/ (20.11.66). On the 21st of November the girl makes a correct reading of *tyckt* by means of substitution in the formerly learnt *tycker*. By the end of the month, the fact that the *c* does not stand for /s/ seems to be clear to her, as *snicka-ren* is read /sni:-kade/ (28.11.66). The function of *ck* to signal a short vowel dominates the two-stage reading of *kvickt* a few days later: /kvi:t . . . kvit/ (4.12.66). Full knowledge is attained at about the middle of December: from that time on only correct readings of *ck* have been noted, e.g. *ryckte* (16.12.66), *packlårarna* (4.1.67), *flugprickar* (4.1.67), *kacklar* (7.1.67), *sträckte* (23.1.67).

ng. That *ng* stands for a single phoneme /ŋ/ is realized rather early. In November and December the combination *ng* is read /n-g/ and sometimes it is immediately converted into /ŋ/: *gung* /gɯ:ng, gɯŋ/ (20.11.66), *hänger* /hɛ:-n-g-er/ (20.11.66), *yngsta* /y:n-g-s-ta, yŋsta/ (16.12.66). The conversion is probably supported by the fact that the word is in the girl's spoken language: on hearing her first incorrect reading she associates it with the spoken word and changes her reading. This might account for the word *ångra* (9.1.67) being read /ån-g-ra/ without conversion, as it was probably not part of the girl's spoken language by that time. After this date, however, no incorrect *ng*-readings have been noted. Thus the correspondence *ng* /ŋ/ seems to be known by the reader at the beginning of 1967.

k and g. Before the autographemes *e, i, y, ä* and *ö* when these correspond to phonemes with heavy stress, the syngraphemes *k* and *g* normally correspond to the phonemes /ç/ and /j/.[84] The more frequent correspondences *k* /k/ and *g* /g/ are perceived quite early (see above p. 87 f.); and, when graphematic reading becomes the normal way of tackling unknown words, *k* is read as /k/ and *g* as /g/ also before the above-mentioned vowels: *kilade* /ki:lade/ (30.10.66), *kör* (verb) /kø:r/ (13.11.66), *utkik* /ɯ:tk-i:k/ (18.12.66), *hedersgäst* /he:ders-gɛst/ (18.12.66).

As early as November—December, however, the first readings with "conversions" appear: *kyrk-* /kyrk-, çyrk-/ (28.11.66), *känn* /kɛn, çɛn/ (30.11.66), *kysste* /kyste, çyste/ (12.12.66), *kinder* /kinder, çinder/ (31.12.66); *get* /ge:t, je:t/ (13.11.67), *gifta* /gifta, jifta/ (12.12.66). These readings continue in January, 1967: *kikade* /ki:kade, çi:kade/ (23.1.67), *bekymmer* /bekymer, beçymer/ (27.1.67), *korgen* /kɔrgen, kɔrjen/ (3.1.67), *gissa* /g-issa, jissa/ (9.1.67).

In January we also find examples where no conversion has been made, like *förgäves* /førg-ɛ:-ves/. In February—March, however, we find the first direct readings of *k* /ç/ and *g* /j/: *kött* /çøt/ (5.2.67), *kissemåns* /çise-mɔns/ (11.2.67), *käx* /çäks/ (23.2.67), *kines* /çines/ (31.3.67), *regera* /reje:ra/ (1.2.67), *general* /jenera:l/ (2.2.67), *bege* /beje/ (2.2.67), *Gärda* /jɛ:rda/ (5.3.67), *Georg* /jetɔr/ (5.3.67), In these readings the rule of the correspondence *k* /ç/, *g* /j/ before the autographemes *e, i, y, ä* and *ö* has been strictly observed. That knowledge of the rule forms part of the reader's competence in February—March is confirmed by the fact that only the pronunciation of *kött* has support in the reader's spoken language: the words *kines, regera, general* and *bege* and the names *Georg*[85] and *Gärda* are not known by the reader; *kisse-(måns)* and *käx* are exceptions from the rule: in standard Swedish they are pronounced /kise/ and /kɛks/.

During the period March, 1967, to February, 1968, sporadic violations of the rule have been noted. Also a few conversions occur. These

---

[84] Exceptions are certain loan-words, such as *kex, gem.*
[85] Besides, *Georg* is not correctly read by the girl.

might, however, be considered as deficiencies in performance rather than lack of competence: *piskkäpp* /pisk-kɛp/ (16.3.67), *kindtänder* /kiːntɛnder, kindtɛnder, çindtɛnder/ (20.6.67), *kiknade* /kiːknade/ (21.2 68), *Gösta* /g-østa/ (5.3.67), *menageri* /mena-geri/ (21.3.67), *generad* /genereːrad/ (20.6.67), *oregerliga* / ɔːregerliga/ (22.2.68), *försiggick* /føːr-sig-gik/ (28.2.68).

After February of 1968 no violations whatever of the rule have been noted.

dj, gj, hj, lj. These four combinations of graphemes all represent the phoneme *j.* In modern Swedish, however, the combinations appear in only a few words. The most common are:

dj: djungel, djup, djur, djävul, djärv, adjö.[86]
gj: gjord, gjort, gjuta.[86]
lj: ljud, ljuga, ljum, ljung, ljunga, ljus, ljuv.[86]
hj: hjort, hjortron, hjul, hjälm, hjälp, hjälte, hjärna, hjärta, hjässa, ihjäl.[86]

The scarcity of such words means that the reader has few chances of ever arriving at the "rule", of ever finding the correspondence *dj* /j/, *gj* /j/ etc.; he just learns the words as glosses when he happens to come across them.

We start with *gj.* In the reading material of 1966 *gjorde* and *gjort* are found many times. On the 21st of March, 1967, when the girl meets *gjuta* she is confounded. She tries four readings /ɧɯːta, çɯːta, gɯːta, g-jɯːta/. The first two of these readings show that the problem of *skj* /ɧ/ and *tj* /ç/ has turned up, it is probably the grapheme *j*, which is part of all three grapheme strings (*gj-, tj-* and *skj-*), which inspires the readings /ç/ and /ɧ/. The last of the readings is a downright graphematic reading: *g* is supposed to represent /g/ and *j* /j/. Although *gjort, gjorde* have been rather frequent in the earlier material—they occur at least five times each during 1966—they cannot function as patterns for the reading of *gjuta;* they have been learnt as glosses, but no rule has been drawn from them.

The same thing is partly true of *dj.* In the reading material of 1966 the word *djur,* its compounds and its inflexions are very frequent. We also meet the word *adjö.* At the end of December, however, when the reader is shown the word *djärva,* she tries to escape the difficulty by changing the word: she reads 1. /dɛlva/, 2. /darva/. One year later she is presented with *djärvaste* and then reads 1. /çɛrvaste/, 2. /jɛrvaste/. The second success-

---

[86] To these words are added derivations like *djurisk, gjutare, ljuvlig, hjälpsam* etc. and inflexions like *djupt, djärvare* etc.

ful reading is no evidence, however, that the reader is aware of the correspondence *dj* /j/; she might just have remembered the word *djärva* and made the adjunction *djärva-ste*. But investigations have shown that the books read in 1967 contain the word *djup*, and, as no note has been taken about the reading of this word, it must have been read correctly. The well-established *djur* affords a much better pattern for the reading of *djup* than for the reading of *djärva*. In fact, the reader needs only to make the substitution *dju/r, -p* in order to arrive at the correct reading. On the other hand, this means that the correct reading of *djup* does not give complete evidence that the reader has really grasped the correspondence *dj* /j/.

The combination *hj-* is met with in three words (with derivations and inflexions) in the books read during 1966: *hjälpa, hjärta* and *hjul*. On the 21st of March, 1967, when the girl is presented with *ihjälstångad*, she reads that word correctly. Probably this is because the patterns are very close; compare *hjäl*pa and *hjär*ta with *ihjäl*stångad. When the reader meets *Hjorten* (31.3.67) and *Hjalmar* (14.4.67), where the patterns are less close, she does not succeed in reading the words. *Hjorten* becomes /hɔrten, çɔrten/, *Hjalmar* becomes /ja:mar, hajmar/; that is, the troublesome combination *hj* is treated in four ways: either the *j* is skipped, or the *h* is skipped, or the two are separated, or *hj* is confused with such combinations of syngrapheme +j as give the pronunciation /ç/—here probably *kj*. On the 14th of April the word *hjärna* is read correctly. This word also has a close pattern, in *hjärta*. After this date there are no notes about *hj*-readings.

Words spelled with *lj* in the books read during 1966 are *ljus, ljusen* and *ljusblå*. On being presented with *ljungen* (5.3.67) the girl reads /ɯŋnen, lɯŋnen, jɯŋnen/. The third reading might be considered a correct rendering, but it could as well be that the *l* is merely skipped in the third reading, just as the *j* has been skipped in the second one. Nor does the correct reading of *lj* in *ljustret* /ju:stret/, more than one year later (22.8.68), give sure evidence that the correspondence *lj* /j/ has been understood. Rather, it is the well-established *ljus* /jɯ:s/ which explains the successful reading—the incorrect pronunciation /jɯ:stret/ (with a long vowel) points in that direction.

tj and *kj*. As a representation of /ç/, *kj* occurs initially in only two Swedish words, *kjol* and *kjortel*.[87] When *kjolar* is presented for the first time (13.11.

---

[87] Apart from the totally obsolete *kjusa*.

66) it is read graphematically /k-j-ɒ:lar/. In July, 1968, the new word *kjortel* is read correctly, probably because of the pattern *kjol*(ar). The girl asks: "Is a 'kjortel' a 'kjol'?" It is to be observed that the reading *Hjorten* /çɔrten/, where *Hj* is probably mistaken for *kj* (31.3.67), suggests that the correspondence *kj* /ç/ is evident to the girl in March, 1967.

In about 20 Swedish words—with compounds, inflexions and derivations—the initial phoneme /ç/ is graphically represented by *tj*: *tjafs, tjat, tjattra, tjeck, tjej, tjo, tjock, tjog, tjuder, tjugo, tjur, tjusa, tjuta, tjuv, tjäder tjäle, tjäna, tjära, tjärn*. In the reading material of 1966 three of these words are represented: *tjattrande, tjocka* and *tjugo*. When *tjöt* is presented (30.11. 66) it is read /tø:t/, *tjäna* (18.12.66) is read /tɛnja/. These two words do not seem to have patterns that are close enough. But not even *tjuta*, whose pattern is the well-established *tjugo*, is read successfully: first it is read /t-j-ɯ:ta/, then this is corrected to /ɧɯ:ta/ (9.1.67). *Tjuta* remains a problem through the whole year: *tjuta* /ɧɯ:ta, t-jɯ:ta, tɯ:a/ (14.7.67), *tjuta* /ɧɯ:ta/ (12.8.67). The reading *gjuta* /çɯ:ta/ (21.3.67) reflects the same problem. Not until the beginning of 1968 does the girl succeed in rendering *tjuta* correctly, and then only on the second try: *tjuter* is read first /ɧɯ:ter/, then /çɯ:ter/ (3.2.68). Two correct readings of *tj* have been made in 1967, however, both in the combination *tju-*: *förtjusning* /førçɯ:tniŋ, førjɯ:tniŋ, førçɯ:sniŋ/, *tjur* /çɯ:r/. But the grapheme sequence remains a problem for a long time: on being presented with the place-name *Tjust* (31.5.68) the girl says: "It is so difficult".[88] In August, 1968, however, the correspondence *tj* /ç/ has probably been realized, as the word *tjällossningen* (25.8.68) is read fluently. Compare, though, the close pattern *tjäna*.

sk, sj, skj, sch, stj. These five graphematic strings all represent the phoneme /ɧ/; *sk*, however only before *e, i, y, ä* and *ö* when these correspond to phonemes with heavy stress, and in the word *människa*.

Not until December 1966 does the girl spontaneously try readings of words beginning in *sk-*. She is then presented with the word *skicka*. On the first try she makes a misidentification, *sticka*. Then she tries to escape the difficulty by skipping the *k* and reading /sika/, finally she suggests *skrika*. Four more readings of words containing *sk* corresponding to /ɧ/ are tried in December. In all four cases the words are read graphematically as if containing /sk/: *skörda* /sk-ø:-rda/ (17.12.66), *skänker* /sk-än-ker/ (18.12.66), *skylla* /sk-ylla/ (27.12.66), *besked* /be-sk-e:d/

---

[88] Unknown names are always difficult as they do not give the same reassuring "feedback" as words which are well known in spoken language.

(31.12.66). These incorrect readings are produced even if there are rather strong patterns for correct readings: with *besked* compare *skeden, matskedar, skena;* with *skylla* compare *skylten, skynda, skymta, skyggar;* with *skänker* compare *skämt, skägg, skällde, skära, skärt.* There are less strong patterns for *skörda: sköt, sköta, sköld* and *skönt.*

Only two more readings of *sk* corresponding to /ɧ/ have been noted, and they are both correct: a successful reading of *solsken* is produced in three stages 1. /sɔl-sken/, 2. /s ɷ:l-ske:n/, 3. /s ɷ:l-ɧe:n/ (11.2.67), and *skötfilten* is immediately read correctly /ɧø:tfilten/ (3.5.67). But these correct readings give no sure evidence that the correspondence *sk* /ɧ/ has been grasped, as *solsken* might as well have been read on the basis of the earlier learnt *sol* and *skena*, and *sköt* (in *skötfilten*) has already been presented as a single word in both September and November, 1966.[89] The three-stage reading of *solsken*, however, contradicts a direct association with *skena;* if the reader had been aware of *skena*, one would have expected a direct reading /s ɷ:lɧe:n/. Moreover, the fact that no reading errors whatever have been noted after February, 1967, concerning *sk* /ɧ/ makes it probable that the reader has by that time become conscious of the correspondence *sk* /ɧ/ before *e, i, y, ä* and *ö.*

From the notes it is not possible to follow the development of the capacity for reading words containing *sj* and *skj*. The word *skjul* is read /sk-juɯ:l/ in October (29.10.66) and that is our last note concerning that graphematic string. As there are, practically speaking, only four words in the Swedish language containing *skj* (*skjorta, skjul, skjuta* and *skjutsa;* with compounds, inflexions and derivations), the matter is of little interest. The words are learnt as glosses, and it is therefore not necessary for the reader to associate *skj* with /ɧ/ in order to become a competent reader of Swedish.

Sjunga is wrongly supposed to be *suga* (21.11.67) and *ansjovis* is read /anjɷ:ves/ (29.4.67). No more notes about *sj* are to be found in the material.

The only pattern in the books read during 1966 for correct readings of *stj* is *stjärnor*, which appears in March and September. This does not help the girl to read *stjälpte* (17.12.66), which is first assumed to be *släppte*, then read *läppte* and finally mistaken for *hjälpte*. In January, 1967, *stjälper* is read graphematically /st-j-ɛlper/ (8.1.67). The first correct reading of *stj* is made in February, when *stjärten*, after the unsuccessful try /jɛrten/, is read /ɧɛrten/ (12.2.67). The reading is facilitated by the

---

[89] This earlier *sköt* is homonymous with *sköt* in *skötfilten*.

very close pattern *stjärnor*; in fact it might be classified as a substitution of "false morphemes": *stjär/n-or, -t-en*. So there is no real evidence that the reader is aware of the correspondence *stj* /ɧ/ in February. The reading /s-t-jɛlkar/ for *stjälkar* in June (21.6.67) shows that the reader is still uncertain. There are no misreadings after that date, however.

The graphematic string *sch* affords problems at the beginning of 1967. The following incorrect readings are made: *schas* /ha:kas/ (8.1.67), *nisch* /nis/ (13.2.67), *mustascher* /mʊstajer/ (10.3.67). *Usch* (15.2.67) is not read at all. Three more readings of *sch* have been noted, and they are all correct: *schaletter* /ɧaleter/ (19.3.67), *planscher* /pl-an . . . plan-ɧer/ (7.4.67), *Äsch* /ɛɧ/ (29.4.67). It is to be observed that all these readings have very close patterns: with *scha*letter compare *scha*s; with plan*scher* compare musta*scher;* and with Ä*sch* compare U*sch*.

x. The grapheme *x* represents a string of phonemes /*ks*/. The first try at reading a word containing *x* is unsuccessful: *telefonväxeln* /telefɔ:n- -vɛ:. . ./ (28.11.66), in spite of the fact that *växte* is part of the girl's reading vocabulary by that time. Other and later readings of four words containing *x* have been noted; all of them are performed correctly, the earliest one on the second try: *taxen* /tasen, taksen/ (23.1.67), *Alexander* /aleksander/ (15.3.67), *uroxar* / ɔksar, rɔksar, ɯ:rɔksar/ (15.3.67), *examen* /ɛksa:men/ (16.3.67). All these words have clear patterns, some of them very close: compare *taxen — saxar; Alexander — sex, extra, exempel; uroxar — talgoxen; examen — exempel, extra.*

This investigation of the grapho-phonematic irregularities has shown that most of them are mastered by the reader during the first half of 1967, that is, within a little more than half a year after the code has been broken. It has also shown that the "rules" are discovered gradually by means of very close patterns which are imitated. Where the material is extensive and the patterns are numerous—e.g. for *k* /ç/ and *g* /j/— observations might be made about the competence and the performance of the reader. It seems as if competence might be a good bit ahead of performance: this means that rules which have obviously been acquired by the reader are violated during a certain period after this competence has been attained.

Chapter Ten
Conclusions. Some additional remarks on intonation, meaningful reading, application, appreciation, writing and spelling

In this study I have shown how a child aged two and a half who is first presented with single words written on cards and then with these words in their linguistic contexts—in books—not only learns the words as entities. Through analyses of, and comparisons between, these acquired words the child gradually succeeds in breaking them up into smaller units—first morphemes, later also graphemes—until she has finally arrived at a full knowledge of the grapho-phonematic correspondences between the written language she is studying and its spoken counterpart. This knowledge enables the child to "transform" any message in the written language she is learning to the corresponding spoken message.

In the case studied, the breaking of the code was accomplished within one year and two months. The time devoted to reading every day varied between 5 and 30 minutes.

In her report Jeanne Chall recommended that the teaching of reading should include the teaching of the code. The sum result of investigation about success and failure in learning to read seems to indicate that the teaching of the code gives better results.

Now, it is to be observed that the children studied in the research work mentioned by Jeanne Chall are school children who start learning to read at the age of five and a half to seven. Might it not be possible that between two and four, the very time when the spoken language is acquired, the child has an extraordinary capacity for absorbing and analyzing language, a capacity that makes the breaking of the code a natural and easy thing? Is it not possible that such a capacity gradually decreases when it has fulfilled its purpose?

In *The Biological Foundations of Language* Lenneberg writes: "There is evidence that the primary acquisition of language is predicted upon a certain developmental stage which is quickly outgrown at the age of puberty" (p. 142). Even if the stage is not totally outgrown until the age of puberty, it seems very likely to me that there must be a gradual weakening of the linguistic capacity from the time when children normally have acquired the grammar of their mother tongue, i.e. from about four years of age.

Thus the capacity should be at its maximum when the child is about two to four years of age, the linguistically most active part of man's life. This seems to be confirmed by modern Continental pedagogical practice with its very early start in foreign- language teaching—in France the *Centre Audio-Visuel* produces material for three-year-old children and these young pupils very soon become fluent speakers of a second language.

If it is true that the capacity for language is greater with children two to four years old than those of six or seven, it is evident that the different groups will not profit equally from being taught by the same methods. As regards the acquisition of foreign languages the following seems to be true:

1. The older the learner the more a "grammatical" method is to be preferred, a method where his attention is drawn to the rules.
2. The younger the learner the more a "direct" method should be used, i.e. a method where he is exposed to the foreign language in natural situations and is allowed to make discoveries for himself, exactly as when he learns his mother tongue. With children two to four years old this method seems to be the only one possible.

What has here been stated about learning a foreign language might also be said of learning to read. The older a learner is the more he may favour a code-learning method. The younger a learner is the more easily he may be able to find the code himself. While a child that starts learning to read when he is six to seven years old might thus profit more from being taught the code parallel with instruction where he is exposed to words in contexts, a child who is two to four years old would be most at ease if he is exposed to the written language in a way that makes it possible for him to learn this in much the same way as he meanwhile learns his first spoken language — i.e. by finding out for himself.[90]

It is easy enough to see the advantages of letting the child find the code himself, while reading books and words from books where the only principle of selection has been to choose literature which is interesting to him and which is written in natural everyday language, where the complexity of the syntax does not too much surpass his own syntactical capacity.[91] Thus the child might at once experience meaningful

---

[90] In the case studied here the girl's joy at finding the code seems to indicate that it was a good and natural way for her; further investigations will show if this holds true also for other children of that age.

[91] See p. 120 about research work in child syntax.

reading, and the principle of application—which is such an important point with the reading-for-meaning supporters—might be satisfied from the very beginning.[92]

It is evident that it is a great advantage for a child at the age of only three and a half both to master the code and to have a reading vocabulary of 1000—1500 words at his command, words that may be recognized immediately without any kind of hesitation or analysis.

In this case study I have concentrated on one aspect of learning to read: the decoding aspect, preferably the finding of the grapho-phonematic correspondences. During the reading sessions I also carefully studied many other aspects of reading, but I shall merely hint at some of the more important observations made.

A. Intonation and phrasing

When the girl had learnt a new set of reading cards, she always read the corresponding book aloud to me. To begin with she was taught to point at every word in order to learn the left-to-right reading habit and not to skip any words. This habit of pointing led to a staccato reading in which the words were pronounced separately with pauses in between.

The girl always reread her books many times, however, and I noticed that when rereading she often abandoned the habit of pointing, and so her phrasing improved. On the 23rd of March she read a new book directly without pointing, and with good intonation and phrasing. From that day on she never pointed and her oral reading constantly improved. At the end of 1966, however, after the breaking of the code, we abandoned the reading cards, and this caused a momentary impairment in connected reading, as the girl was forced to read a lot of new words directly in context without first having practised them on reading cards. After about six months of practice, however, she was able to read "*a prima vista*" rather fluently, with a natural intonation and phrasing.

I never taught the girl intonation. Here too I allowed her to discover for herself. It seems that much of this discovering was made when she reread the books. I sometimes noticed her sitting practising different intonations and stress patterns when rereading the books aloud to herself. On the 10th of May, 1966, she read about a duck that had left its pond and walked to the sea. Scared by the big waves the duck said: "*Min damm är bättre den*" ("My pond is better"). She read the passage over

---

[92] About early application see p. 117 f.

a couple of times, finally choosing the stress pattern "*Mín damm . . .*", with the stress on the possessive pronoun.

On the 11th of February, 1967—after three months of direct, connected reading without reading cards—the child read a book aloud about a girl called Sarah. She then made a self-correction which showed that she was good enough at decoding to be able to pay attention to intonational details. The following sentence appeared: " '*Det är faktiskt en blåmes*' *sa Sara tyst för sig själv*". (" 'It really is a blue tit', said Sarah silently to herself"). She started to read the sentence in a normal voice but stopped before "Sara"—and then reread Sarah's retort whispering.

On the same day the girl also corrected her own reading when she had once failed to give the right tonal pattern indicating the end of a sentence and to pause after the punctuation finishing it. Four months later, on the 22nd of June, 1967, I got the first evidence that her correct phrasing was not merely intuitive, that she was really conscious of the function of punctuation. Rereading an old book aloud she suddenly stopped at the end of a sentence. "Here is a *dot*", she said, making a big pause. She then read the rest of the book most carefully, making the pauses after the different punctuation marks extra long.

The girl also speculated over the function of capitals. At the beginning of October, 1966, she observed that the first word of a sentence was printed with a capital; in April, 1966, she asked why a certain word, *VÄNTA* ("wait"), was printed all in capitals (the author here had wanted to indicate that somebody was tired of waiting).

As a proof of the keen attention of infants I might also mention that no misprints of earlier learnt words escaped the girl's attention. *Babar* written as *Barbar* was immediately corrected (23.2.1967) and the misprint *söng* for *sjöng* was noted at the first reading (26.12.1967).

B. Active reading

On all levels the girl's reading was a very active one. As soon as she met a word she did not understand she asked me about its meaning. She often criticized the language in the books. Dialectal word-forms or stylistical variants deviating from her own use were considered to be "wrong" or "ugly". She often made small changes in the syntax when reading: changes of word order, additions of words in elliptical expressions etc. Also here she seemed to adapt the text to suit her own language or the language she was used to hearing. A typical example is when (March 1st, 1967) "*ett svårt göra*" (a difficult job) was changed to "*svårt att göra"* (difficult to do) because the girl had never before heard *göra* used as a noun.[93]

From the very beginning the girl intimately connected *reading and reality*. New words on reading cards were often, in the girl's comments, put in relation to known linguistic and non-linguistic contexts.

Ex. *seglade* (sailed) June 10th, 1966. *"Vilka var det som var ute och seglade nu förresten, hos faster Else?"* (Who are out sailing now, at Aunt Else's?).

Larsson (proper noun) July 2nd, 1966. *"Den lilla bebens pappa som bor härborta, han heter Larsson, å hennes morfar han e lite barskallig"* (The little baby's father living down there, he is called Larsson, and her (the baby's) grandfather is a bit bald.).

målade (painted) July 5th, 1966. *"Vem är det som målar? Morfar till exempel."* (Who is painting? Grandfather for instance.).

såld (sold) September 8th, 1966. *"Det kanske är min vagn som har blitt såld; att jag inte behövde den."* (Perhaps it is my pram that has been sold; for I did not need it.).

The girl also criticized the contents of what she was reading, testing them against her own experience of life. Reading about Babar's marriage she said: "Why should he get *married?* An elephant!" (Feb. 2nd, 1966). Reading in *Bullerbyboken* about the children who were impatiently waiting for Christmas and who said that waiting turned their hair grey, the girl commented: "That is not what gives people grey hair. It is only when they get old" (9.4.1967).

Naturally, reading was experienced as more meaningful when the girl read about things that were well known to her from real life. But I have also witnessed that when she had first read about certain things and phenomena in her books, her later experience of the thing in real life became much more intense and rich than it would probably have been without the literary anticipation. Thus her first sunset, experienced in August, 1967, was a sheer delight; and the first time she saw cows grazing she was in a rapture, stopped and shouted in a voice full of joy: "Oh, this must be a *pasture!"* The sunsets and pastures of literature had finally come to life.

The girl's books also inspired her non-verbal life in many other respects. She often introduced scenes from books into her games, building houses after having read *The New House*, constructing roads for her

---

[93] About such corrections of the texts see R. Söderbergh, *"Strukturer och normer i barnspråk"* (1968).

cars after having read *The New Road*. Last but not least, she identified herself with all the heroes of the literature she read.

The problem of fiction and its relation to reality was very keen to her. When, at the age of three years and nine months, she was reading the Dutch author Ninke van Hichtum's book about Mother Afke's ten children she asked: "Have these people really *existed?*" "Possibly", I said. "Yes", she replied, "for if so, we will meet them in Heaven and then they can teach us to speak Dutch."

C. Appreciation

The most advanced stage of literacy, according to the reading-for-meaning supporters, has been reached when literature can be both *applied* and *appreciated*. We have just seen a few examples of application, and I will now go on to illustrate that even a very small child reading by itself may appreciate literature.

A favourite book was *The Children's Bible* by Anne de Vries. I noticed that the girl often stopped her oral reading of the Bible after having finished a very dramatic passage, and then she went over this passage again, silently. On the 21st of October, 1967, at the age of four and a half, the girl had read about the crucifixion. She went back and reread the passage telling how Jesus asks St. John to take care of his mother Mary and be like a son to her ("When Jesus therefore saw his mother, and the disciple standing by, whom he loved, he saith unto his mother, Woman, behold thy son! Then saith he to the disciple, Behold thy mother! And from that hour that disciple took her unto his own home".) She then said: "*Det här var en fin liten dikt. Mittemellan det hemska var det en fin liten dikt*". (This is a fine little poem. In the middle of all the frightful things there is a fine little poem.)

D. Writing and spelling

At about the age of three and a half the girl began trying to write letters herself. For some reason she concentrated on the capitals. By June of 1967 she could write all capitals except B, J, M, N, Q, U, V and X; in July only X was still missing, and she then also failed to write G and Y. On the first of November, 1967, I tested her again and found that she then could write the whole alphabet, capitals and versals. By that time she had also begun to write little missives to invented persons.

When the girl was four and a half her spelling had already become remarkably good. Now, at the age of seven and a half,[94] she simply knows how to spell and needs not devote any time to learning how. This skill, which is normally attained only after many years of hard school work, had come to her quite unconciously as a by-product of her early reading. Would it not be a good thing if all children had this experience: of learning to read as easily as they learn to talk and of learning to spell without knowing that they are learning how; of having attained full literacy at an age when children normally begin to learn the ABC? During the first school years a lot of time and hard work is now being devoted to acquiring the elementary skills of reading and spelling. With these skills already at the pupil's command there could be time for more meaningful and stimulating work and activities at school. Thus still more could be made of the wonderful, receptive and harmonious years before puberty.

[94] She now (autumn, 1970) is in the 3rd class of the lower stage in the Swedish Basic School (klass 3 på grundskolans lågstadium).

Chapter Eleven
Suggestions for further investigation

This study has been carried out on one single child. The next thing that should be done is to test many children, let us say 100 to 150. This should be done by a team of linguists and psychologists.

The only child studied in this treatise was learning written Swedish. It would be of great interest to find out how other written languages are acquired. Swedish is an inflectional language with several regular bound morphemes which are spelt phonematically. These will help the reader to discover very soon for himself the correspondences between phonemes and graphemes. English, however, is very different in this respect, -s being one of the few phonematically spelt morphemes. It seems probable that finding out the system would be more difficult work in English than in Swedish. On the other hand, Finnish, which is a highly inflectional language and which has an almost phonematical spelling, should afford ideal conditions for discovering the code.

Before a study is carried out on many children, it would be a great advantage to have more knowledge about the young child's linguistic development. In research work now being done at the University of Stockholm, we examine the syntactical development of Swedish children from the appearence of the first two-word sentences (age 1 1/2 to 2) until all the basic syntactic structures are acquired (age 3 1/2 to 4). When this research work is finished we will be able to construct reading material that is suited to the actual linguistic capacity of children from two to four years of age. This material could then be used with the experimental group of 100 to 150 children mentioned above.

At the end of the experiment—and also at intervals in later life— the experimental group of 100 to 150 children ought to be tested to give us information about the effects of early reading. How does early reading affect general linguistic development as manifested in pronunciation, vocabulary, syntax, ability to understand oral/written information, ability to give an oral/written account of something that has happened; ability to discuss, to argue, to solve problems etc.? One might also test the influence of early reading on secondary linguistic abilities such as writing and spelling. Last but not least: what does early reading mean to a child's willingness to cope with written material and to its love of books?

It seems to me that early reading along the lines suggested in this study might help retarded children in their linguistic and general development. Perhaps this method could be used with children born deaf—if the spoken explanation of words is replaced by pictures and film, possibly also by situations in real life where the teacher writes down what is happening.[95]

Thus there are numerous tasks involved in further investigation on this subject. As I see it, there is great hope that both normal and retarded children might benefit from this approach to attaining literacy, where learning to read is defined as learning a w r i t t e n l a n g u a g e and where the learner is therefore exposed to suitable reading material at the age when s p o k e n l a n g u a g e is normally acquired—not acquired because the environment imposes language upon the child at that age, but because the child has then reached a biological stage where his preparedness for language is at its prime.

[95] Investigations on the language acquisition of deaf children are carried out by a team in Uppsala, headed by Karl-Georg Ahlström.

SWEDISH-ENGLISH GLOSSARY

This glossary contains all Swedish words (and inflexional forms of words) treated in the book, except names. The translations given refer to the contexts from which the Swedish words have been taken, for the most part children's books. The sign * before a Swedish word means that the word has been coined by the child.

adjö *interj.*, goodbye 108
affär (-en) *n.*, shop 30
alla *pron.*, all 90
allihop *pron.*, all, everybody 41, 94
alltihop *pron.*, everything 94
ank|a (-or-na) *n.*, duck 68
ansikte (-t) *n.*, face 96
ansjovis *n.*, anchovy 111
ap|a (-an, -or) *n.*, monkey 53, 103
att *conj.*, that 34; *before infinitive* to 117; (*för*) ~ because, for 117
av *prep.*, of, by 9, 90

back *adv.*, back 52
backe (-n) *n.*, hill 53
bada *v.*, bathe, have a bath 55, 59
baka *v.*, bake 89
bakåt *adv.*, backwards 97
balkongdörr (-ar) *n.*, balcony door 97
ballong (-er-na) *n.*, balloon 30
banta *v.*, slim 59
bara *adv.*, only, just 33, 34, 85
barskallig *adj.*, bald 117
bebe (-n-s) *n.*, baby 117
bege *v.*, ~ *sig* depart 107
behöv|a (-de) *v.*, need 75, 100, 117
bekymmer *n.*, care, anxiety 107

berg *n.*, mountain 45, 82, 83
berätta *v.*, tell 93
besked *n.*, answer, information 110
bestäm|d (-t) *adj.*, fixed, clear, determined 61
bil (-ar-na) *n.*, car 45, 68
bild (-er-na) *n.*, picture 69, 73
björkris *n.*, birch twigs 65
bland *prep.*, among 80, 88
blek *adj.*, pale 79, 80, 81, 87
blev *v.*, *past tense*, got, became 80
bli (-r) *v.*, get, become 21, 80, 88
blivit, blitt *v.*, *past part.* got, become, been 117
blomm|a (-or-na) *n.*, flower 30, 63, 68, 80
blåmes *n.*, blue tit 116
blås|a (-er) *v.*, blow 80, 88
bo (-r, -tt) *v.*, live, dwell 83, 117
bok *n.*, book 83
boll (-ar) *n.*, ball 31, 68, 80, 90, 91
bonde (-n) *n.*, farmer 45
bord (-et) *n.*, table 45
bort *adv.*, away 33
bortskämd *adj.*, spoilt 33
brev *n.*, letter 45
bror *n.*, brother 30; *broren the brother 30

bruka (-r) *v.*, use to 47
brum *interj.*, buzz 81, 88, 92
*brummihjul (nonsense word) 88
brätte *n.*, brim 53
bu *interj.*, boo 81
bukett *n.*, nosegay, bouquet 75
bur *n.*, cage 81
busk|e (-ar) *n.*, bush 75
by (-n) *n.*, village 34
byggnadsställning *n.*, scaffold 97
byrå *n.*, chest of drawers 84
byt|a (-t) *v.*, change 83
båda *pron.*, both 55, 59
bäck (-en) *n.*, brook 29, 37
bäddning (-en) *n.*, bed-making 75
bära *v.*, carry 85
bäst (-a) *adj.*, *sup.* best 61
bättre *adj. comp.*, better 115
börja (-de) *v.*, begin 65
*börjis (nonsense word) 65

cembalo *n.*, harpsichord 83
cement *n.*, cement 91, 95
copyright *n.*, copyright 83
cykel *n.*, cycle 83, 91
cykla (-r, -de) *v.*, cycle 90, 91

dag (-ar) *n.*, day 21, 80, 83, 88; *i ~
    today* 21
dags *adv.* (*det är*) ~ (it is) time 59
dala (-r) *v.*, decline 90, 91
damm *n.*, pond 115, 116
dansa (-de) *v.*, dance 34
de, dom, *pron.*, they 34, 65, 103
dem *pron.*, them 25
den *pron.*, it 28, 72, 115, 117; *def.-
    art.*, the 72, 117
det (de) *pron.*, it 21, 25, 33, 34, 116,
    117; that 28; there 118; ~ *har
    inte den* that one hasn't 28; ~
    här this 118; *def.art.*, the 72
dikt *n.*, poem 118
diskbänk (-ar) *n.*, sink 93, 106
djungel *n.*, jungle 108
djup (-t) *adj.*, deep 108, 109
djur *n.*, animal 108, 109

djurisk *adj.*, animal, bestial 108
djärv (-a, -are, -aste) *adj.*, bold 108,
    109
djävul *n.*, devil 108
drog *v.*, *past tense*, drew, pulled 60
du *pron.*, you 21, 27, 33
dumbom (-s) *n.*, fool 27
dunig (-a) *adj.*, downy 65, 88
då *adv.*, then 62
där *adv.*, there 25
dö (-r) *v.*, die 47
dörr *n.*, door 47

egen *adj.*, own 96
egentligen *adv.*, properly 96
ej *adv.*, not 91
ek *n.*, oak 70, 80, 89
ekorr|e (-ar-na) *n.*, squirrel 70, 80
elektriker *n.*, electrician 92, 96
elektrisk (-a) *adj.*, electric 95, 97
elva *num.*, eleven 60
en, ett *indef.art.*, a, an 9, 21, 116,
    118
enda *adj.*, only 60
examen *n.*, examination 112
exempel *n.*, example 112; *till* ~ for
    instance 117
explosion *n.*, explosion 77
extra *adv.*, extra 112

faktiskt *adv.*, really 91, 92, 116
fall *n.*, case 91
fanns *v.*, *past tense*, was, existed 91
fara *v.*, go, travel 85
farbror (pl. farbröder) *n.*, uncle;
    man 91
fasa *n.*, horror 91
*faskitisa (nonsense word) 91
fast *adv.*, firmly 91
faster *n.*, aunt 117
fat *n.*, dish 83
fet (-a) *adj.*, fat 91
fin (-t, -a) *adj.*, fine 65, 91, 118
finn|as (-s) *v.*, exist, be 31
fisk *n.*, fish 23

fjäril (-ar -na) n., butterfly 30, 63, 101

flamma n., flame 103

flick|a (-an, -or) n., girl 32, 64, 68

flitig (-a) adj., busy 88

flugprickar n., fly-specks 106

flyga v., fly 88

flyt|a (-er, -ande) v., float 74

flyttkarl (-ar-na) n., remover 103

fort (-are) adv., quickly 72

*fortade (nonsense word) 72

fortfarande adv., still 95

fot (-en) n., foot 91

fotboll n., football 31

fotografi n., photo 27, 28

fram adv., along 33

fru (-n) n., wife, woman 32

frukt n., fruit 85, 91, 95

frys|a (-er) v., be cold, feel cold 33

fråga (-r, -de) v., ask 65, 68, 88

fröken n., miss 101

fyra num., four 94

få (-r) v., get, receive 65, 91; *vi får let us* 25

fåg|el (-lar-na) n., bird 30, 63

färdig (-a) adj., ready 88, 94

färg n., colour 32, 94

färghandel (-n) n., colourman's shop 32

fönster n., window 64, 78

fönsterruta n., window-pane 64, 78

för prep., for 64; to 116; *without corresponding word in English* 21

förarhytt (-en) n., driver's cabin 92, 96

för att conj., to, in order to 34

före prep., before 64

förgäves adv., in vain 107

förr adv., before 83

förresten adv., by the way 117

försiggick v., past tense, took place 108

förstod v., past tense, understood 61

förstörd adj. part., destroyed 61

förtjusning n., enchantment 110

gammal (-t) adj., old 95, 97; *gamla* 90

gasta v., shout 102

gata n., street 83, 102

ge (-r) v., give 27, 65, 83

generad adj., embarrassed 108

general n., general 107

genom prep., through 94

*genomhus (nonsense word) 94

gest n., gesture 83

get (-en-s) n., goat 72, 107

gifta v., ~ *sig* marry 107

gilla (-r) v., like 90

gissa v., guess 107

gjord, gjort v., *past part.*, made, done 108

gjorde, v., *past tense*, made, did 108

gjuta v., cast 108, 110

gjutare n., founder, moulder 108

glad adj., happy, glad 72

glass n., ice-cream 37

glömm|a (-er, -de) v., forget 34

god (-a) adj., good 100

gott adv., good 83

gran (-en) n., fir; christmas tree 34

grann|e (-ar) n., neighbour 88

grind (-en) n., gate 79, 81

grinvarg n., whimperer 88

gris n., pig 79, 92

*grisden (nonsense word) 79, 81

grod|a (-or-na) n., frog 30, 63, 88

grund (-en) n., foundation 96

gråta v., weep 81, 102

gräs (-et) n., grass 72, 88

gräshopp|a (-n) n., grasshopper 88

grön (-t, -a) adj., green 72, 78, 81, 88

*grönen (nonsense word) 72, 81

gröt (-en) n., porridge 72, 81

gul (-a) adj., yellow 90

gumma n., old woman 88

*gummahjul (nonsense word) 88

gummihjul n., rubber-tyred wheel 88

gung interj., swing 106

jag *pron.*, I 21, 33, 64, 88, 91, 117
jo *adv.*, yes, but yes 101
ju *adv.*, but 33; of course, surely 91
jul *n.*, Christmas 34, 37, 65; (*i*) *julas* (last) Christmas 37
julklapp (-en, -ar-na) *n.*, Christmas gift 31
juste *adj.*, all right, correct 83
jättefin *adj.*, superfine 9
jätterolig (-t, -a) *adj.*, great fun 69

kackla (-r) *v.*, cackle 106
kagge *n.*, keg, cask 104
kak|a *n.*, cake; biscuit 55, 59, 89
kalv (-en) *n.*, calf 90
kanin (-er) *n.*, rabbit 33
kanske *adv.*, perhaps 117
kapp|a (-or) *n.*, coat 95, 103
katt *n.*, cat 83
kattung|e (-ar-na) *n.*, kitten 30, 63
kela (-r) *v.*, pet 90
kika (-de) *v.*, look 107
kila (-r, -de) *v.*, run, scamper 52, 92, 107
kind (-er) *n.*, cheek 107
kindtänder *n.*, molar teeth 108
kines *n.*, Chinaman, Chinese 107
kissemåns *n.*, pussycat 107
kittla (-r) *v.*, tickle 52
kjol (-ar) *n.*, skirt 109, 110
kjortel *n.*, skirt 109, 110
kjusa *n.*, glen, dell 109
klapp (-ar) *n.*, pat 31
klapp|a (-ar, -ade, -ande) *v.*, pat 65, 68, 72, 74
klia (-r) *v.*, scratch 52
klippa *v.*, cut 89
klistra (-de) *v.*, paste 95
kliv|a (-er) *v.*, walk, step 45
klocka *n.*, watch 30
*klockaffär (-en) *n.*, the watchmaker's 29
klunk (-ar) *n.*, draught, sip 47
klut *n.*, patch, rag 103
knorra *v.*, murmur, grumble, 100
ko (-r-na) *n.*, cow 93, 101

kol *n.*, coal 83
komm|a (-er) *v.*, come 34, 66, 83
korg (-en) *n.*, basket 107
korkmatt|a (-or) *n.*, linoleum 93, 95
kossa (-n) *n.*, cow 101
kosta (-r) *v.*, cost 31, 101
*kostan (nonsense word) 101
kras *n.*, gå i ～ go to pieces 100
krasch *interj.*, crash 100
kring *prep.*, round, around 34
kudde *n.*, pillow 21
kull|e (-en, -ar) *n.*, hill 72, 75
kullerbytt|a (-or) *n.*, somersault 75
kunde *v.*, *past tense*, could 45
kvack *interj.*, quack 100, 101
kvalitet *n.*, quality 9
kvick (-t) *adj.*, quick 106
kvitt *interj.*, chirp 89, 90
kväll (-en) *n.*, evening 34, 99
kyla *n.*, cold 83
kyrka *n.*, church 34
kyrk- *n.*, of the church, church- 107
kyss|a (-te) *v.*, kiss 107
kåsör *n.*, causerie-writer 84
känn|a *v.*, feel 107
kärr *n.*, marsh 83
käx *n.*, biscuit 107
köpa *v.*, buy 32, 83
kör|a *v.*, drive 107
kött *n.*, meat 107
köttbullar *n.*, meat balls 92

lade *v.*, *past tense*, put, laid 90
lag *n.*, law 83
laga (-de) *v.*, mend 72, 88, 90
lager *n.*, layer 95
lakan *n.*, sheet 90
land *n.*, country 100
landshövding (-en) *n.*, governor 75, 100
*landshövningen (nonsense word) 75, 100
lapa (-r) *v.*, lap, sap, lick 52, 90
lapp *n.*, patch 53
larm (-et) *n.*, noise 55, 59
lat (-a) *adj.*, lazy 53, 54

leda *v.*, lead, guide 94

lek *n.*, play 80, 81, 87

lek|a *v.*, play 89

len (-a) *adj.*, soft 94, 103, 104

leta *v.*, seek 61

ligga *v.*, lie 88

lik (-a) *adj.*, like 25, 89

likadant *adv.*, the same 95

likna (-r) *v.*, be like 24, 25; compare 25

lilla see liten

lillebror *n.*, little brother 30

lite *adv.*, a bit 117

liten (lilla, små) *adj.*, little, small 22, 33, 72, 89, 90, 117, 118

liv *n.*, life 59

ljud *n.*, sound 108

ljuga *v.*, tell a lie 108

ljum *adj.*, tepid, lukewarm 108

ljung (-en) *n.*, heather 108, 109

ljunga *v.*, flash 108

ljus (-et, -en) *n.*, light; candle 108, 109

ljusblå *adj.*, light blue 109

ljust|er (-r-et) *n.*, fish-gig 109

ljuv (-t, -a) *adj.*, sweet 108

ljuvlig *adj.*, sweet, lovely 108

lov *n.*, permission 59

lurvig (-a) *adj.*, shaggy 65, 88

lys|a (-te) *v.*, shine 76

låna (-t) *v.*, lend, borrow 59

lång (-t) *adj.*, long, tall 59

lås *n.*, lock 104

låt|a(-er) *v.*, let 47

lägenhet (-en) *n.*, flat 95

lägg|a (-er) *v.*, lay 81, 90

läggdags *adv.*, time to go to bed 90

lämna (-de) *v.*, leave 90

*längde (nonsense word) 81, 90

länge *adv.*, long 81, 90

*läppte (nonsense word) 111

lära *v.*, learn; teach 85

läs|a (-er) *v.*, read 22, 31, 64, 78

läslapp *n.*, reading card 21

lät *v.*, *past tense*, let 103, 104

lös (-t, -a) *adj.*, loose 60, 61

löv (-en) *n.*, leaf 90

mage *n.*, stomach 24, 26, 48

mala *v.*, grind 83

mamm|a (-an-s, -or-na) *n.*, mother 21, 24, 27, 28, 32, 64, 68, 73, 89

mark (-en) *n.*, ground 82, 89, 90

mat *n.*, food 82

matsked (-ar) *n.*, tablespoon 111

matt *adj.*, weak, faint 82

mattläggare *n.*, carpet-layer 85, 95, 103

med *prep.*, with 28

men *adv.*, but 22, 72

menageri *n.*, menagerie 108

middag *n.*, dinner 33

mig *pron.*, me 27

mil *n.*, mile 45

min (-a) *pron.*, my 31, 117

mittemellan *adv.*, in the middle of 118

mjuk (-a) *adj.*, soft 72, 89

morfar *n.*, grandfather 21, 117

morgon (-en) *n.*, morning 79, 81

mormor *n.*, grandmother 21, 23, 79

motorcyk|el (-l-ar) *n.*, motor-cycle 91

mugg *n.*, mug, jug 37

mun *n.*, mouth 37

murare *n.*, bricklayer 95

mus *n.*, mouse 82

musikkår *n.*, band, orchestra 81

mustascher *n.*, moustaches 112

måla (-r) *v.*, paint 117

måltid *n.*, meal 89, 92

månad (-er) *n.*, month 76

många *pron.*, many 76

*mångare (nonsense word) 76

mä *interj.*, baa 102

människa *n.*, man, human being 110

märk|a *v.*, notice 83, 84

mätte *v.*, past tense, measured 48, 100

mörk (-a) *adj.*, dark 51, 83

mörk|er (-r-et) *n.*, darkness 51

ned, ner *adv.*, down 27, 28
nisch *n.*, niche 112
nog *adv.*, probably 32
nosa (-de) *v.*, sniff, smell 72
nu *adv.*, now 83, 117
ny (-a) *adj.*, new 50, 51, 94
när *adv.*, *conj.*, when 21, 22, 25, 33
nära *adv.*, near 85
nästa *adj.*, next 64
nästan *adv.*, almost 84

och (å) *conj.*, and 28, 33, 72, 105, 117
ofta *adv.*, often 31
oj *interj.*, oh 91
om *conj.*, if; *adv.*, again 76
*omlysa (nonsense word) 76
ompysslad *v.*, *past part.*, nursed, coddled 76
oregerlig (-a) *adj.*, unmanageable 108
orgel (-n) *n.*, organ 34
ost (-en) *n.*, cheese 101

packlår (-ar-na) *n.*, packing-case 106
paket *n.*, parcel 83
pall (-ar-na) *n.*, stool 73
papp|a (-or-na-s) *n.*, father, daddy 24, 25, 26, 33, 48, 78, 89, 91, 101, 117
park (-en) *n.*, park 82, 89, 91, 92
parkeringsplatser *n.*, parking places 75, 97
*parkningsplatser (nonesense word) 75
pengar (-na-s) *n.*, money 30, 62, 63, 68
piller *n.*, pill 100
pinne *n.*, peg 89
pippi *n.*, dicky, bird 89
piskkäpp *n.*, whip 99
*plack (nonsense word) 100
plansch (-er) *n.*, plate, illustration 112
plask|a *v.*, splash 73, 95, 101
plommon *n.*, plum 85, 92, 95

plötsligt *adv.*, suddenly 85, 93, 95
pojk|e (-en, -ar-na) *n.*, boy 30, 32, 73
prat *n.*, talk, chat 53, 54
prata *v.*, talk, chat 53, 54
precis *adv.*, exactly 24, 25, 26, 27, 48, 91
på *prep.*, of 9, on, in 21, 72

rad *n.*, row 83
radio *n.*, wireless 9
ramp *n.*, foot-lights 52
regera *v.*, reign 107
ren (-t, -a) *adj.*, clean 104
ruckel *n.*, ramshackle house 91, 96, 106
rulla (-r) *v.*, roll 90
rum *n.*, room 81, 88, 92
rund (-a) *adj.*, round 45
rut|a *n.*, pane 64
ryck|a (-te) *v.*, jerk, pull 106
råka (-de) *v.*, meet 72, 74
rädd *adj.*, frightened, afraid 21
rätt (-er) *n.*, meal 53
räv *n.*, fox 90

sa *v.*, *past tense*, said 21, 116
saga *n.*, tale 88
sal *n.*, hall 83
samma *pron.*, the same 28
sax (-ar) *n.*, scissors 112
schalett (-er) *n.*, kerchief 112
schas *interj.*, scat 112
se (-r) *v.*, see 64
segla (-de) *v.*, sail 117
sex *num.*, six 112
sig *pron.*, himself, herself, itself, themselves 37
sil *n.*, strainer 59
sin *pron.*, his, her, its, their 37, 59
silver *n.*, silver 45
sjunga *v.*, sing 34, 111
själv *pron.*, myself, yourself, himself, herself, itself 60, 116
sjö (-n) *n.*, lake 91
sjöng *v.*, *past tense*, sang 116

skall v., pres., shall, will 27
sked (-en) n., spoon 47, 111
skena v., bolt, run away 47, 111
skicka v., send 110
skjort|a (-an, -or) n., shirt 111
skjul (-en) n., shed 96, 111
skjuta v., shoot 111
skjutsa v., drive, take 111
skog (-en) n., wood, forest 44, 46, 47
skola (-n) n., school 44, 46, 47
skorpa n., biscuit 93
skranglig (-a) adj., lank, lathy 88, 89, 91
skrapa (-r) v., scrape 89, 91
skrek v., past tense, cried, shouted 89, 94
skrika v., shout 110
skrubba (-r) v., scrub, scour 89
skulle v., past tense, should, would 33
skutta (-de) v., jump 72, 75
*skuttningen (nonsense word) 75
skygg (-a) adj., shy, timid 88
skygga (-r) v., take fright, start 111
skylla v., accuse 110, 111
skylt (-en) n., sign board 111
skymta v., catch a glimpse of 111
skynda v., hurry 111
skynke (-t) n., cloth, curtain 27
skägg n., beard 45, 111
skäll|a (-de) v., bark 111
skämt n., joke 111
skänk|a (-er) v., give 110, 111
skär (-t, -a) adj., rose, pink 45, 111
sköld n., shield 111
skön (-t) adj., beautiful 111
skörda v., harvest, reap 110, 111
sköt v., past tense, shot 64, 111
sköta v., nurse 64, 111
skötfilt (-en) n., baby blanket 111
slag n., ett litet ∼ for a short time 34
slag n., kind; ∼ s kind of 59
sluta (-t) v., finish, end 95
slutligen adv., finally 95, 97
sluttning (-en) n., slope 75

släp n., work, toil 103, 104
släpp|a (-te) v., let go 111
slätt n., field 53
smaka (-de) v., taste 72, 89
små see liten
smådjur n., small animals 95
sned (-a) adj., crooked, warped 95
snickare (-n) n., carpenter 106
snurr|a (-or-na) n., wind-mill 30
snår (-en) n., brush, thicket 104
snäll (-t, -a) adj., kind 31, 63, 65, 90
sol n., sun 111
solsken n., sunshine 111
som pron., who, which, that 33, 69, 117; adv., conj., as 27
somliga pron., some 69, 88
son n., son 83
sopades v., past passive, was swept 93
sov|a v., sleep 31, 68
spela (-r) v., play 90
spis (-ar) n., kitchen range 95
spring|a (-er, -ande) v., run 74
*springland (nonsense word) 74
spår n., track 82
stad (-en) n., town; stan the town 34
stanna (-r) v., stay 33, 64
stek n., steak 94
sticka v., knit 110
stilig adj., elegant 97
stjälk (-ar) n., stalk 112
stjälp|a (-er, -te) v., turn over, upset 111
stjärn|a (-or) n., star 32, 111, 112
stjärt (-en) n., tail 111, 112
stock (-ar-na) n., log 106
stor adj., big, great 100, 104
*storet (nonsense word) 100
storrengöring n., house-cleaning 104
strå (-na) n., straw 72
sträck|a (-te) v., stretch 106
studs|a (-ade) v., bound, rebound 68
stygg (-a) adj., bad, wicked 50, 51, 94

styra v., steer 94
stå (-r) v., stand, be 41; say 21
stång (-en) n., pole 85
ställning (-ar) n., stand, scaffold 95, 97
stöta v., push 74
stött v., past part., offended 103
suga v., suck 111
svår (-t) adj., difficult 116
så (-dde) v., sow 95, 103
så adv., so 21, 103; then 72; ~ hår like this 22; often without a corresponding word in English 24
såg v., past tense, saw 41
såld v., past part., sold 117
säga v., say 88
säl n., seal 83
sätta v., put 93
sönder adj., broken 48, 49, 50, 51

ta (-r) v., take 27; ~ fram 'dem' show 'dem' to me 25; ~ ner take down 27
tablett (-er) n., tablet 94
tack interj., thanks 52, 100
tacka (-r) v., thank 52
tak (-et) n., roof 9
tal n., number 83
tala (-de, -t) v., speak, talk 72
talgoxe (-n) n., great tit 112
tam adj., tame 103
tapeter n., wallpaper 94, 95
tappa (-r) v., drop 70
tass (-ar-na) n., paw 30, 63
tax (-en) n., badger-dog 112
telefon (-er-na) n., telephone 73
telefonväxel (-n) n., telephone switch 112
till prep., to, for 33, 34
titta (-r) v., look 64
tjafs n., chatter 110
tjat n., teasing, worrying 110
tjattr|a (-ande) v., babble, chatter 74, 110
tjeck n., Czech 110

tjej n., girl, lass 110
tjo interj., ho 110
tjock adj., thick, fat 110
tjog n., score 110
tjuder n., tether 110
tjugo num., twenty 110
tjur n., bull 110
tjusa v., enchant 110
tjut|a (-er) v., cry 110
tjuv n., thief 110
tjäder n., capercailzie 110
tjäle n., the frost in the ground 110
tjällossningen n., the breaking up of the frost in the ground 110
tjäna v., serve 110
tjära n., tar 110
tjärn n., tarn 110
tjöt v., past tense, cried 110
toff|el (-l-or-na) n., slipper 73
tog v., past tense, took 60
torka v., wipe, dry 50, 51, 89
tramp|a (-ar) v., tramp, trample 99
trasslig (-t) adj., tangled 95
tre num., three 24, 65; e de tre stycken there are three of them 24
trehjuling n., tricycle 65
tretton num., thirteen 83
trevlig (-a) adj., nice 88
trilla (-r) v., fall 90
tro (-r) v., believe 50, 51
tung adj., heavy 49, 50, 51
tunga n., tongue 22
tunnel n., tunnel 49, 50, 51
tusen num., thousand 95, 101
tvätt n., wash 58
tyck|a (-er, -t) v., think 106
tyst adv., silently 116
tå (-r-na) n., toe 93, 94
tårta n., cake 93
tält n., tent 90

uggla (-n-s) n., owl 30, 31
ullig (-a) adj., woolly 88
undra (-r) v., wonder 48
uppför prep., up 72

ur *prep.*, out of 101
urox|e (-ar) *n.*, aurochs 112
usch *interj.*, faugh, oh 112
ut *adv.*, out 64, 78
ute *adv.*, out, outside, outdoors 64, 117
utkik *n.*, lookout 107

vack|er (-er-t, -r-a) *adj.*, beautiful 90
vad *pron.*, what 21, 22, 90
vagn *n.*, pram 117
valp (-ar) *n.*, puppy 80
var *adv.*, where 90
var *v.*, *past tense*, was, were 33, 34, 72, 90, 117, 118
vara *v.*, be 85
varann *pron.*, each other 90
varje *pron.*, each, every 90
varken *conj.*, neither 90
varm (-t, -a) *adj.*, warm, hot 55, 59
vatt *n.*, watt 83
vatten *n.*, water 90
vecka (-n) *n.*, week 106
vem *pron.*, who 117
verkstäder *n.*, workshops 95
vet|a *v.*, know 21, 83, 90, 91; *vet du do you know* 21
vett *n.*, sense 82
vi *pron.*, we 22, 33, 34, 90
vidare *adv.*, on, onwards 72
vilk|en (-a) *pron.*, who, which 117
vind (-a) *adj.*, crooked 95
vissla (-r) *v.*, whistle 74, 91
visste *v.*, *past tense*, knew 74
vit (-t) *adj.*, white 83, 89
våg (-or) *n.*, wave 88
vår *n.*, spring 90
våt (-a) *adj.*, wet 63
väg (-ar) *n.*, way 80
väl *adv.*, well 65
väldig (-t) *adj.*, mighty; great, huge 65

välta *v.*, tilt over 90
vän *n.*, friend 69
vänlig (-a) *adj.*, friendly 69
vänta *v.*, wait 116
vätt *v.*, *past part.*, wetted, damped, moistened 83
väx|a (-te) *v.*, grow 112

yngsta *adj.*, youngest 85, 106
yxa *n.*, axe 83

zebra *n.*, zebra 83

åk|a (-er, -te) *v.*, go, drive 72, 74
åker (-n) *n.*, field 32
ångra (-r, -de, -t) *v.*, regret 107
ångvält (-en) *n.*, steam-turbine 99
år (-et) *n.*, year 82
åter *adv.*, back, again 47
återigen *adv.*, again 75
*återningen (nonsense word) 75
åtta *num.*, eight 81, 102

ägg *n.*, egg 81, 90
älg *n.*, elk 45
äng *n.*, meadow 45
är (e) *v.*, *pres.* am, are, is 21, 24, 28, 116
ärt (-er) *n.*, pea 51
äsch *interj.*, never mind 112
ät|a (-er) *v.*, eat 23, 33, 51

ög|a (-on) *n.*, eye 24, 26, 48, 79
önska (-r) *v.*, want, wish 91
öva *v.*, practise; *dom ~r sig they are practising* 34, *~ sig i å sjunga practise singing* 34
över *adv.*, *prep.*, over 90

BIBLIOGRAPHY

Allén, Sture. 1965. Grafematisk analys som grundval för textedering. Acta Universitatis Gothoburgensis. Göteborg, Nordistika Gothoburgensia 1.
Allén, Sture. 1967. Forhållandet mellan skrift och tal. Språk, språkvård och kommunikation. Lund, Sweden.

Bloomfield, Leonard. 1942. Linguistics and reading. Elementary English Review 19.125–30, 183–86.
Bloomfield, Leonard. 1963. Language. New York, Holt, Rinehart and Winston.
Brantberg-Frigyes, Birgitta. 1969. Kan en treåring lära läsa. Lund, Sweden, Gleerups.
Brown, Robert and **Colin Fraser.** 1963. The acquisition of syntax. In: Verbal behavior and learning: Problems and processes. Proceedings of the 1961 (2nd) Conference on Verbal Learning and Verbal Behavior, Ardsley-on-Hudson, N.Y. Edited by: Charles Norval Cofer and Barbara S. Musgrave. New York, McGraw-Hill.
Brown, Roger and **Ursula Bellugi.** 1964. Three processes in the child's acquisition of syntax. In: New directions in the study of language. Edited by Eric H. Lenneberg. Cambridge, Mass., The M.I.T. Press.

Chall, Jeanne S. 1967. Learning to read: The great debate. New York, Mc-Graw-Hill.
Chomsky, Noam. 1969. Aspects of the theory of syntax. Cambridge, Mass., The M.I.T. Press.

Dahlstedt, Karl-Hampus. 1965. Homonymi i nusvenskan. Nysvenska Studier.
Doman, Glenn. 1964. How to teach your baby to read: The gentle revolution. New York, Random House.
Dravina, Velta (Ruke). 1963. Zur Sprachentwicklung bei Kleinkindern. Beitrag auf Grundlage lettischen Sprachmaterials. Lund, Sweden.

Elert, Claes-Christian. 1970. Ljud och ord i svenskan. Stockholm, Almqvist and Wiksell.
Erdmann, B. and **R. Dodge.** 1898. Psychologische Untersuchungen über das Lesen. Halle, E. Germany.

Flesch, Rudolf. 1955. Why Johnny can't read—and what you can do about it. New York, Harper and Row.

Francis, W. Nelson. 1962. Graphemic analysis of late Middle English manuscripts. Speculum XXXVII. 32–47.

Fries, Charles C. 1963. Linguistics and reading. New York, Holt, Rinehart and Winston.

Gates, Arthur I. 1968. Strømninger i tiden. Published by Landsforeningen af Laesepaedagoger on the occasion of the Second World Congress on Reading, Copenhagen, August.

Gelb, Ignace J. 1963. A study of writing. Chicago, University of Chicago Press. Revised edition.

Gleason, Henry A., Jr. 1961. An introduction to descriptive linguistics. New York, Holt, Rinehart and Winston. Revised edition.

Gleason, Henry A., Jr. 1965. Linguistics and English grammar. New York, Holt, Rinehart and Winston.

Hayakawa, Samuel Ichiyé. 1959. Language in thought and action. London, Allen and Unwin. Third edition 1972, New York, Harcourt Brace Jovanovich.

Hockett, Charles F. 1958. A course in modern linguistics. New York, Macmillan.

Huey, Edmund Burke. 1968. The psychology and pedagogy of reading. Cambridge, Mass., The M.I.T. Press. First published 1908.

Kavanagh, James F., ed. 1968. Communicating by language: The reading process. Proceedings of the 1968 Conference on Communicating by Language, The Reading Process, New Orleans. Bethesda, Md., National Institute of Child Health and Human Development. Washington, D.C., Superintendent of Documents, Government Printing Office.

Lenneberg, Eric H. 1967. Biological foundations of language. New York, Wiley.

McCarthy, Dorothea. 1954. Language development in children. In: Manual of child psychology, second edition. Edited by: Leonard Carmichael. New York, Wiley.

Menyuk, Paula. 1969. Sentences children use. Cambridge, Mass., The M.I.T. Press. Reading Research Quarterly. 1965/66. Newark, Delaware.

Sigurd, Bengt. 1965. Phonotactic structures in Swedish. Lund, Sweden, UNISKOL.

Sigurd, Bengt. 1967. Språkstruktur. Stockholm, Wahlström och Widstrand.

Smith, Frank and **George A. Miller,** eds. 1966. The genesis of language. Cambridge, Mass., The M.I.T. Press.

Söderbergh, Ragnhild. 1968. Strukturer och normer i barnspråk. Nordisk Tidskrift.

Stauffer, Russell G. 1969. Teaching reading as a thinking process. New York, Harper and Row.

Uldall, Hans Jørgen. 1944. Speech and writing. Acta linguistica hafniensia (Copenhagen) 4.11–16.

Wardhaugh, Ronald. 1969. Reading: A linguistic perspective. New York, Harcourt Brace.

Wiegand, C. F. 1907. Untersuchungen über die Bedeutung der Gestaltqualität für die Erkennung von Wörtern. Zeitschrift für Psychologie und Physiologie der Sinnesorgane.

Zeitler, J. Tachistoskopische Untersuchungen über das Lesen. Wundt's Philosophische Studien. Leipzig 1881–1903. Bd. XVI.

Printed books used as reading material in the experiment Dec. 1965 to Dec. 1966.

Ainsworth, Ruth o. **Ridout, Ronald,** Den lilla geten. Svensk Läraretidnings förlag 1965.

———— En anka på äventyr. Svensk Läraretidnings förlag 1965.

———— Lek med mig. Svensk Läraretidnings förlag 1965.

———— Rullbandet. Svensk Läraretidnings förlag 1965.

Baker, Marybob o. **Miller, J. P.,** Det snälla lejonet. FIB 1965.

Beim, Jerrold o. **Källström, Ylva,** Bollen som kom bort. Rabén o. Sjögren 1965.

Fujikawa, Gyo, Djurens barn. Illustrationsförlaget 1964.

Heilbroner, Joan o. **Chalmers, Mary,** Mamma fyller år. Illustrationsförlaget 1962.

Higgins, Don, Jag är en flicka. FIB 1966.

———— Jag är en pojke. FIB 1966.

Hughes, Shirley, Lisas och Toms dag. Berghs 1965.

Janus Hertz, Grete o. **Leo-Hongell, Veronica,** När Lisa och Lena hade röda hund. Rabén o. Sjögren 1965.

Meeks, Esther K. o. **Pekarsky, Mel,** Kossan Kajsa. Illustrationsförlaget 1960.

Peterson, Hans o. **Källström, Ylva,** Den nya vägen. Rabén o. Sjögren 1965.

———— Det nya huset. Rabén o. Sjögren 1966.

———— Gubben och kanariefågeln. Rabén o. Sjögren 1960.

Pfloog, Jan. Kattboken. FIB 1965.

Proysen, Alf o. **Stödberg, Nils,** Byn som glömde att det var jul. Rabén o. Sjögren 1962.

Risom, Ole, Kajsa Skogsmus. FIB 1965.

———— Kalle Kanin. FIB 1965.

Selsam, Millicent E. o. **Lobel, Arnold,** Fias Fjärilar. Illustrationsförlaget 1962.

Sigsgaard, Jens o. **Ungermann, Arne,** Katinka och dockvagnen. Rabén o. Sjögren 1965.